RANDOM HOUSE

masterpiece

crosswords

edited by
STANLEY NEWMAN

VOLUME

1

TIMES
BOOKS

dedication

To my parents, Claire and Jerry Newman of Delray Beach,
Florida, who bought me my first almanac.

ISBN 0-8129-6373-3

Text design by Julia Reynolds and Stanley Newman
Manufactured in the United States of America
4   6   8   9   7   5   3

introduction

Recently a lady from Long Island wrote me at *The New York Times* complaining that the puzzles I edit there have "too many long words." She said, "It must be easier to construct such puzzles – long horizontal blanks and words leading down from them."

In my reply I said I hoped she would come to realize, after more thought, how *incredibly difficult* such puzzles are to produce. Any able crossword constructor can interlock three-, four-, and five-letter words. Crisscrossing longer words in an open pattern containing a high percentage of white squares takes considerably more skill because each word has more junctions to be dealt with.

Constructions with many long words, moreover, are not empty exercises in an arcane art. They make for better solving. Crosswords with mostly three-, four-, and five-letter words tend to repeat the same answers again and again. No matter how cleverly OBI, ERIE, and ALE are clued for the 67th time, you still have a feeling of déjà vu about the answers. The wide-open patterns, on the other hand, bring in fresh, new vocabulary, and when well done add considerable spice to solving.

The above letter points up the need for a course in Puzzle Appreciation 101, such as the book you're now holding, because many solvers, I think, don't know what to look for in a crossword.

Editor Stanley Newman has commissioned 50 puzzles from America's top puzzlemakers, edited them in the medium- to medium-hard range of difficulty, and has written "liner notes" on each constructor's work. He tells you who the puzzlemakers are, explains how their minds work, and spotlights the notable or remarkable aspects of the results.

When you're done with this book, I hope, you will not only have enjoyed the puzzles, but will have a better understanding of why you did – and you'll be better able to recognize and appreciate quality crosswords wherever they appear.

Will Shortz

editor's acknowledgments

What makes a crossword a masterpiece? The same qualities that go into the making of a luxury automobile or a fine painting, such as the superior talents of the creators, and the meticulous attention paid to every detail. The people who have worked with me in the realization of this book not only personify the *Masterpiece* concept, but have added immeasurably to it by their participation. Thanks to:

- Harold Clarke, president of Random House Value Publishing, for sharing the dream, and coining the name *Masterpiece Crosswords*
- Peter Osnos, publisher of Times Books, for his unflagging support from day one
- Julia Reynolds, for designing and typesetting the manuscript
- Naomi Osnos, for her counsel on the interior design
- Robbin Schiff and Claudine Guerguerian, for their elegant cover
- Eli Hausknecht, for her help in selecting the paper and binding
- Nancy Inglis, for copyediting all the nonpuzzle prose
- Jon Delfin and Martha Trachtenberg, for proofreading the manuscript
- Will Shortz, for the introduction
- And the puzzlemakers, for creating the masterpieces you are about to experience

After you've completed these puzzles, I hope you'll want to look for additional puzzles by *Masterpiece* contributors. They can be found in the publications mentioned herein, such as *The New York Times*, *Newsday*, and *Games* magazine. For subscription information on Mel Rosen's Crosswords Club or my Uptown Puzzle Club, call 1-800-874-8100.

In addition, the *Times* and *Newsday* crosswords are available to America's newspapers through syndicated services. If you're not happy with the crossword running in your local paper, you have the power to change things. Write to the features editor and make your feelings known.

Please let us know how you like *Masterpiece*. The address: Times Books Puzzles & Games, 201 East 50th Street #11-1, New York, NY 10022. We'll be happy to respond personally if you include a self-addressed stamped envelope.

Stanley Newman
Managing Director, Puzzles & Games
Times Books

stanley newman

Crossword creator and editor, managing director of puzzles & games for the Times Books division of Random House, Inc. Home: New York

Previous Occupations
College teacher (mathematics and statistics), market-research analyst, Wall Street computer consultant and bond analyst.

Education
B.S. in mathematics from Brooklyn College, M.S. in statistics from Rutgers University.

Crossword Credentials
First U.S. Open Crossword Champion (1982). Founder and President of the American Crossword Federation. Editor and publisher of two puzzle magazines: *Tough Puzzles* (1983-1994) and *Tough Cryptics* (1992-present). Editor of more than 25 crossword collections in book form for various publishers. Editor of the nationally syndicated Newsday Crossword since 1988. Editor for the Uptown Puzzle Club since 1993. Creator of the crosswords that appear in *People*, *Health*, *Sport*, and *America West* magazines.

Puzzle #1 - "That's Entertainment"
A puzzle similar in style to the ones I create for *People* magazine – over 70 percent of the clues relate to showbiz! One thing that makes this puzzle different from the 13x13 *People* crosswords: the 14x14 diagram. Virtually all published crosswords have an odd number of squares on each side, because the symmetry (with one central row and column) is easier for constructors to work with than that in even-numbered ones (with two central rows and columns). I selected this "odd" even size to accommodate the 14-letter name of a Hollywood notable and the title of a recent film he starred in.

Puzzle #2 - "21-Gun Salute"
Another "theme-packed" puzzle, but of a different kind. The subject matter is much more restrictive than the showbiz focus of #1. There were only 37 possible theme answers to choose from; I managed to cram in over half of these.

Puzzle #3 - "The Human Equation"
A pretty diagram, thanks to its left-right symmetry in addition to regular symmetry (where the diagram looks the same if turned upside down). Over 100 possible theme entries had to be examined to find the eight actually used.

One of the things I think makes puzzles more fun is lively phrases in nontheme answers. I was able to fit over a dozen of them in this puzzle. Watch your step – a few of these are tricky!

Puzzle #4 - "Diagramless"
Diagramlesses are the crosswords I most enjoy creating, because I'm not restricted to a rectangular shape and can put black squares wherever I like. My diagramlesses generally have lots of long words and "wide-open" patterns (with large areas of white space). This puzzle has a theme, inspired by 51 Across – too tempting to pass up. The theme answers are symmetrically placed, but will not all be found in the longest answers.

Here are a few tips for diagramless tyros:

- Start 1 Across in the second column.
- 1 Across must have seven letters, because the second Across clue is numbered 8.
- Because the second and third answers Across (8 and 9) have no correspondingly numbered Down answer, they must be entered directly underneath 1 Across.
- Fill in one black square to the left and right of each Across answer, and above and below each Down answer.
- The puzzle obeys the same symmetry rules as standard crosswords.
- At least one answer word will touch each of the four borders of the diagram.

1
that's entertainment
by stanley newman

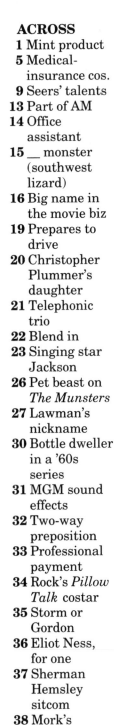

ACROSS
1 Mint product
5 Medical-insurance cos.
9 Seers' talents
13 Part of AM
14 Office assistant
15 __ monster (southwest lizard)
16 Big name in the movie biz
19 Prepares to drive
20 Christopher Plummer's daughter
21 Telephonic trio
22 Blend in
23 Singing star Jackson
26 Pet beast on *The Munsters*
27 Lawman's nickname
30 Bottle dweller in a '60s series
31 MGM sound effects
32 Two-way preposition
33 Professional payment
34 Rock's *Pillow Talk* costar
35 Storm or Gordon
36 Eliot Ness, for one
37 Sherman Hemsley sitcom
38 Mork's superior

39 Fiber-rich substance
40 Actress MacGraw
41 Subway in a jazz tune
44 Entertainment conglomerate
48 High-budget film starring 16 Across
51 Emulate Greg Louganis
52 Hugh O'Brian TV role
53 In the center of

54 St. Moritz backdrop
55 Petty clash
56 "__ Lisa" (Nat King Cole tune)

DOWN
1 All-star team, perhaps
2 __ *Is Not Enough* (Susann novel)
3 Start of a Spillane title
4 Brokaw and Jennings

5 Silent screen star?
6 *Les* __ (Broadway blockbuster, familiarly)
7 "__ to Billie Joe" (#1 tune of '67)
8 Pennant-winning team in *Damn Yankees*
9 *Doctor Dolittle* actress
10 Give autographs

11 Beseeched
12 Gilbert of *Roseanne*
17 Bee, on *The Andy Griffith Show*
18 Sends forth
22 "And where's that soggy plain?"
23 Mutt's colleague
24 "Zip-__-Doo-Dah"
25 "I __ Your Love Tonight" (Elvis tune)

26 MTV reporter Tabitha
27 Comediennes Arthur and Benaderet
28 Singer Guthrie
29 New Kids on the Block fan
31 Barbara Cartland books
34 TV personal-finance advisor Dolan
35 *The Firm* author
38 *Havana* star
39 *Psycho* sicko
40 Take as one's own
41 *Betsy's Wedding* director and star
42 *An American* __ (animated film)
43 Answer an invitation
45 Mason's role in *20,000 Leagues Under the Sea*
46 Moran of *Happy Days*
47 Luke Skywalker's teacher
49 *This Is Spinal* __ (rock-parody film)
50 *Sliver* author Levin

2

21-gun salute

by stanley newman

ACROSS

1 Diamond lady
4 Attack word
7 Side of a doorway
11 #36
14 Ugandan exile
15 Brooklyn or Manhattan, for short
16 Site of a Perry victory
17 *Hollywood Squares* win
18 #8
20 #13
22 Throw out a line
23 It may be convertible
25 __-doke
26 Methuselah's father
28 Possible reason for an R rating
29 "Managed care" insurance org.
31 #11
32 #10
33 #39
37 __ Arbor, MI
38 Manage somehow
39 Realtor's favorite sign
41 *Happy Days* network
42 Elapse quickly
43 Short journey
44 Prefix for structure
46 Burkina Faso neighbor
48 #18
50 De __ (erstwhile Chrysler car)
51 #37

52 Papa preceder
53 Hyannisport haul
54 Unspecified person
55 Name in Yugoslavian history
57 Accrue
59 #35
62 #28
64 Health-spa feature
66 Debussy contemporary
67 Mandela's org.
68 TV trophy
69 Cameraman's concern

70 Org. cofounded by Jane Addams
73 Airport lessee
74 Hit on the head
75 #30
78 #9 or #23
82 Showtime rival
83 Singer Jacques
84 Prolific love poet
85 Personal
86 Mentalist's claim
87 Requirement
88 Soufflé ingredient

89 Unopened in the box

DOWN

1 Max's costar in *The Emigrants*
2 Muckraker Tarbell
3 #16
4 Impose an order on?
5 Wrath
6 Type of piano
7 #3
8 Oratorio solo
9 1000 G's
10 Loudness unit
11 "See here, . . ."

12 Use a drill
13 Kangaroo kid
15 #41
19 Throw one's support behind
21 Tie up a boat
24 Metal-in-the-rough
26 Clean-air agcy.
27 "Smoking or __?"
28 Swindle
29 Powerful acid, symbolically
30 #4
32 Fool (with)
34 #27

35 Source of hydroelectric power in Spain
36 Elvis' record label
38 #42
40 Make a choice
42 '20s Broadway nickname
43 He's radio-active
45 Blynken's buddy
46 Skirt style
47 Kerrigan maneuver
48 Understood
49 #26 or #32
51 ERA supporter
53 Iran-contra org.
56 Mag for small business
57 Shamus
58 Even a little bit
59 #7
60 Winter bug
61 Ends a match early
63 Bellow in the library
65 "What __ bid?"
66 Burt Reynolds' ex
69 #38
70 Yearn
71 Cygnet sires
72 Computer-programming technique
73 Long time
74 Sea cell
76 One of the Dow Jones Industrials
77 *Red River* actress
79 Mean, in brief
80 Be beholden to
81 Compass pt.

the human equation

by stanley newman

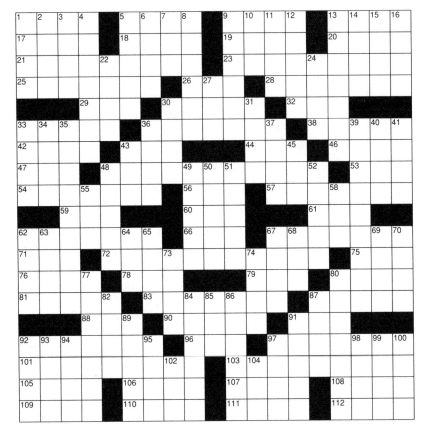

ACROSS

1 Wedding-cake section
5 Famous last word
9 "__ Lisa"
13 Tinsel Town forecast
17 Stare at
18 Comics marsupial
19 First shepherd
20 Out-of-airport transport
21 PROTESTORS - T = recent candidate
23 BASTILLE + G = software tycoon
25 Level of achievement
26 Pilot's heading: Abbr.
28 Bargain-basement
29 Porker's pad
30 December songs
32 President pro __
33 Pond plant
36 Unfair attack
38 Twangy-sounding
42 Lone Star coll.
43 Orchestra's place
44 Crest competitor
46 Application datum
47 Part of MST
48 TERMINATES + V = comic actor
53 Hammarskjöld's predecessor
54 Temperamental sort
56 Mash product
57 Gentleman, perhaps
59 Erstwhile Mideast nation: Abbr.
60 In days of yore
61 Set, as a trap
62 Where shorts are worn to work
66 Object of Aztec reverence
67 Said with confidence
71 Fancy vase

72 FEARSOME-LY + R = investigative reporter
75 "__ Got a Crush on You"
76 Architect __ van der Rohe
78 Tale's subject, at times
79 Put a strain on
80 Chick's tail?
81 Employee's extras
83 Expect
87 Brandish
88 Part of TGIF
90 Biblical poem
91 Not from the US
92 Pseudo-'50s rock group
96 René's OK
97 John Wayne film of '70

101 SEPTILLION - S = memorable politician
103 LENINISM + O = playwright
105 Bow-carrying god
106 Bone-dry
107 *Peter Pan* beast
108 Screenplay direction
109 Toon skunk Le Pew
110 Football great Rote
111 "30 days __ September . . ."
112 Spanish number or French adverb

DOWN

1 Rocky hills
2 "__ the sun in the morning . . ."

3 Designer Schiaparelli
4 Prepares for a big day
5 Silly stuff
6 Oliver Twist's request
7 Self-perception
8 "Ask me later!"
9 Phone company, familially
10 Kimono accessory
11 Singer Carter
12 Dedicate
13 Jeff Bridges sci-fi film of '84
14 Buddy, in Brisbane
15 The yoke's on them
16 Main point
22 Some stock options

24 Lola in the *Damn Yankees* film
27 Tree Planters' State: Abbr.
30 Punishment for a kid
31 What high spirits do
33 Noticeably opulent
34 Name of four German kings
35 UNDERTREAT - A = media mogul
36 Didn't come clean
37 Cleverness
39 RESIDUALLY - U = astronaut
40 "What __ mind reader?"
41 Sly look
43 Grade-sch. supporter
45 Abbr. on a cassette-recorder jack

48 Blood component
49 Clear the blackboard
50 Motown's first #1 tune
51 Very long time
52 L.A. King, for example
55 Ark occupant
58 Viking ships had one
62 Dislodge, in airline-speak
63 Source of the Niagara River
64 Wally Cleaver portrayer
65 All lined up
67 Worshiper's place, maybe
68 Irritate
69 First name in daredeviltry
70 Monopoly prop
73 Great __ Forward ('50s Mao program)
74 Literally, "indivisible"
77 Hope's nickname
80 '48 blockade beater
82 Jazz-band leader Kenton
84 Wagner heroine
85 Sigma follower
86 Draw back
87 Apt rhyme for "pursues"
89 Take surreptitiously
91 Take surreptitiously
92 Conforming, with "in"
93 Bring on board
94 Each
95 Light and thin, as material
97 Something hysterical
98 Peer of Ike and Hap
99 Be an omen of
100 Unnamed folks
102 Mae role of '28
104 Pitcher's pride

4

diagramless

by stanley newman

ACROSS

1 The original Renaissance man
8 First __ (collectible book)
9 Fights against
10 Mighty insect
13 Santa __, CA
14 Wings: Lat.
15 Mick Jagger, for one
21 Corn container
25 Perrier rival
26 Famous work by 1 Across
28 Classified information?
31 Carpentry groove
33 __ voce
34 Strike-zone boundary
35 Biblical birthright barterer
36 Tuileries, *par exemple*
40 Rijksmuseum favorite
46 Expect again
51 What you're doing at the moment
57 Engineer's assistant
58 Contemporary expressionist
59 Bath baby carriage
61 Simone's state
62 16,000-line epic poem
67 Cop __
72 Decline to bid
73 Home deliveries of a sort

78 Magnificent workmanship
79 *Look Back in* __
80 TV-tube gas
81 Quite content
86 Dionysus' dad
87 A quarter of tetra-
88 Flow away
89 Dashes' relatives
93 Like sandals
94 Abstract giant

DOWN

1 Shut out
2 *A Bell for* __
3 Of prime importance
4 Communications conglomerate
5 Not even one
6 Former mile-run record holder
7 Those elected
10 Hgt.
11 Wynonna Judd's mom
12 Carpenter's projection
14 In __ (agitated)
16 *My Name Is Asher* __ (Potok book)
17 Noted lithographer
18 Robert De __

19 NAFTA forerunner
20 One of the Siamese twins
21 What a tartan symbolizes
22 Nuptials, for one
23 "Nothing but blue skies do __"
24 Opera villain, usually
27 Genesis creation
28 *My Camera in Yosemite Valley* creator
29 Second thoughts
30 Soak (up)
31 Medical word form
32 En route to Maui, perhaps
37 Field of conflict
38 LP, e.g.
39 A barrel of laughs
41 Ring judge
42 *Exodus* hero
43 *All Things Considered* radio network
44 Tool's partner
45 Office sub
47 Begone's beginning

48 Seek, as a price
49 Equi- kin
50 With 52 Down, kind of garage
52 See 50 Down
53 Early afternoon
54 Moreno's namesakes
55 Gene makeups
56 Marine drillers: Abbr.
60 Ginnie __ securities
62 "A fish __ animal who swims in a brook . . ."
63 Sicilian simoleons
64 Absorbed by, as a hobby
65 Opposing, to Jed Clampett
66 Negative prefix
68 O'Neill output
69 Actress Olin
70 Coop group
71 Calculus calculation
74 Ultimate degree
75 Dine on the lawn?
76 Unhurried, amiable personality
77 Tee shot's path
82 Alehouse
83 Breathers?
84 Kicks in
85 Botch
89 "The racer's edge"
90 Upsilon follower
91 Big bird of myth
92 Concert's conclusion

a.j. santora

Semiretired construction-company worker. Home: Massachusetts

Previous Occupation
Construction-company owner.

Education
High-school graduate.

Crossword Credentials
First appeared in *The New York Times* in 1948 (a Sunday puzzle – daily crosswords didn't start in the *Times* until 1950). Widely published in puzzle magazines and syndicated crosswords; most prolific in 1960s and '70s. Won first prize in a nationwide contest held for crossword constructors in 1980.

With a puzzlemaking career nearing the half-century mark, A.J. Santora is the veteran among *Masterpiece* constructors. Even his earliest *Times* puzzles bear the distinctive touches that today are Santora trademarks, such as wide-open diagrams (large areas of white squares) and liberal use of contemporary idioms and names out of today's news.

The most impressive thing about Santora's puzzles is his ambitious placement of theme answers – often "stacked" (two adjacent) or intersecting each other. This is much more difficult than it might sound. A constructor's task of finding theme answers of the same length (because of symmetry requirements) is difficult enough. Finding pairs of theme answers that can symmetrically "stack" (yielding workable letter combinations in the other direction) or intersect (having a common letter in symmetrical locations) takes an immense amount of patience.

Santora himself believes that his building-construction background has a lot to do with his approach to puzzlemaking. Whether that's true

or not, A.J. Santora has truly earned the title "constructor's constructor."

Puzzle #5 - "Wanted Poster"
Puzzles with wide-open spaces like these (note the big blocks of words in each of the four corners) are almost always themeless. But there are an amazing six theme answers here – four of them intersecting.

Puzzle #6 - "Motivational Quote"
A five-part quotation with a clever play on words; the name of the quote's author and a place associated with the author both intersect the central part of the quote.

Puzzle #7 - "Down the Garden Path"
A dazzling diagram – note the pairs of stacked theme answers at 14 and 15 Down and 12 and 18 Down. The broad-based clues range from mythology to current TV series.

Puzzle #8 - "Surnaming"
A tour de force, with an amazing *six* intersecting theme answers, and nontheme subjects covering the past (41 Across), present (76 Across), and future (30 Across).

5
wanted poster
by a.j. santora

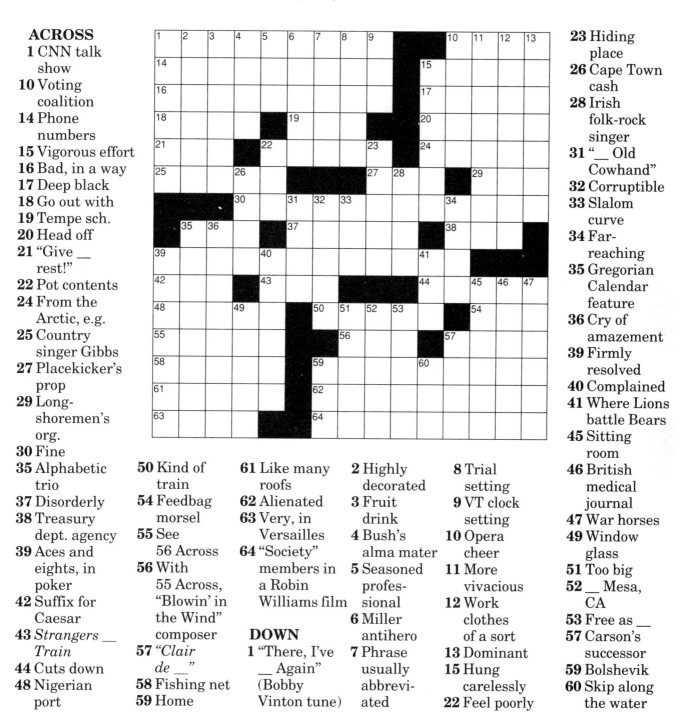

ACROSS

1 CNN talk show
10 Voting coalition
14 Phone numbers
15 Vigorous effort
16 Bad, in a way
17 Deep black
18 Go out with
19 Tempe sch.
20 Head off
21 "Give __ rest!"
22 Pot contents
24 From the Arctic, e.g.
25 Country singer Gibbs
27 Placekicker's prop
29 Long-shoremen's org.
30 Fine
35 Alphabetic trio
37 Disorderly
38 Treasury dept. agency
39 Aces and eights, in poker
42 Suffix for Caesar
43 *Strangers __ Train*
44 Cuts down
48 Nigerian port
50 Kind of train
54 Feedbag morsel
55 See 56 Across
56 With 55 Across, "Blowin' in the Wind" composer
57 "*Clair de __*"
58 Fishing net
59 Home
61 Like many roofs
62 Alienated
63 Very, in Versailles
64 "Society" members in a Robin Williams film

DOWN

1 "There, I've __ Again" (Bobby Vinton tune)
2 Highly decorated
3 Fruit drink
4 Bush's alma mater
5 Seasoned professional
6 Miller antihero
7 Phrase usually abbreviated
8 Trial setting
9 VT clock setting
10 Opera cheer
11 More vivacious
12 Work clothes of a sort
13 Dominant
15 Hung carelessly
22 Feel poorly
23 Hiding place
26 Cape Town cash
28 Irish folk-rock singer
31 "__ Old Cowhand"
32 Corruptible
33 Slalom curve
34 Far-reaching
35 Gregorian Calendar feature
36 Cry of amazement
39 Firmly resolved
40 Complained
41 Where Lions battle Bears
45 Sitting room
46 British medical journal
47 War horses
49 Window glass
51 Too big
52 __ Mesa, CA
53 Free as __
57 Carson's successor
59 Bolshevik
60 Skip along the water

6
motivational quote
by a.j. santora

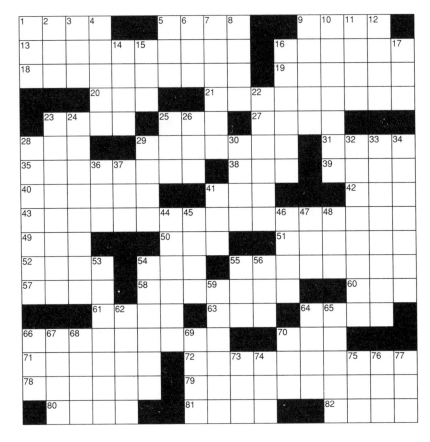

ACROSS

1 Icelandic saga
5 Metric prefix
9 "Phooey!"
13 Burr's best-known role
16 Beethoven piece
18 START OF QUOTE
19 Personal preferences
20 Guileful
21 PART 2 OF QUOTE
23 Jubilation
25 Ernesto Guevara
27 Gaelic
28 "All the Things You __" (Kern tune)
29 Sharply curved
31 Breathing sound
35 Song sections
38 *Cakes and __*
39 Book after Joel
40 Directing job
41 Architectural wing
42 Mornings: Abbr.
43 PART 3 OF QUOTE
49 __ Simbel (Egyptian ruins site)
50 Bit of British legalese
51 Work shoe
52 Uncommon, to Cato
54 Cold-weather bug
55 Some pots and pans

57 Comic-strip distribution org.
58 Plaintiff, perhaps
60 C. Everett Koop's colleagues
61 List-making official
63 Bout-stopping result
64 Spanish ayes?
66 PART 4 OF QUOTE
70 In honor of
71 Goren's game
72 END OF QUOTE

78 Inspired
79 Computer error message
80 Dangerous snakes
81 Burns or Barrie
82 Either Holbein

DOWN
1 Center starter
2 Telephonic trio
3 Thirsty
4 Came to mind
5 Patriotic soc.
6 Pilot's dir.

7 Award, as a degree
8 One against
9 Thorough-fares
10 "__ fool according to his folly": Proverbs
11 French comic actor
12 Proofreader's word
14 Holiday season
15 Spring time
16 *Tristram Shandy* author
17 Blonde shade

22 Comedian Charles Nelson __
23 City associated with 33 Down
24 What an outstretched arm signals
25 Preserve, in a way
26 __ *Girl Friday* (Cary Grant film)
28 Payment problem
29 Goes quickly
30 Seer's reading
32 Mixtures

33 Football coaching great and quote source
34 Dead Sea Scrolls writers
36 The old college cry
37 Half a Heyerdahl title
41 Apocrypha bk.
44 Champaign footballers
45 ". . . three men in __"
46 Mitch Miller's instrument
47 Keats subject
48 Auto gear
53 Made sense
54 Not quite perfect
55 Sort
56 '20s Flying Cloud was one
59 Racial
62 Noses out
64 Just fair
65 Kind of coffee
66 Agent's employer
67 Film role for Shirley
68 Some soul food
69 Danson and Weems
70 Entertainment
73 Chinese religious doctrine
74 Driver's lic. stat
75 Strain __ gnat
76 Fall from grace
77 Banquet introducers

7

down the garden path

by a. j. santora

ACROSS

1 Baseball clubs
5 Circumference
10 Channels 14 and up
13 Circus star
16 Jollity
17 Painter Chagall
19 Poetic pause
20 World-weary
21 Met melodies
23 Cows chew them
24 Mr. Lugosi
26 Tennis coup
28 Red ink
29 __ apso
32 Safecracker, in slang
34 Suffix for scram
36 Business-name alias: Abbr.
37 AFL's partner
38 "Dies __"
40 Printer's proofs
42 Liq. meas.
43 Toward the stern
44 Lounge around
45 Algerian port
46 Word on a krone
48 Solicitous attention: Abbr.
49 Straw, essentially
50 Indonesian island
51 "Doe, __, a female . . ."
52 __ and aahs
54 Adjust the alarm clock
55 New Haven trees
56 Don't give up
57 Lose freshness
59 Wee bit
60 __ Green (onetime elopers' haven)
62 Gen. Robert __

63 Consequently
65 "__ You Lonesome Tonight?" (Elvis tune)
66 Football great Graham
68 Colonial official
69 Complaint, so to speak
70 Actress Ward of *Sisters*
72 World Series mo.
73 More than enough
74 Sitarist Shankar
75 Line of clothing?
76 Electrical unit

77 Engineer's deg.
78 Silents star Renee
80 "__ bigger and better things!"
81 Citrus drink
82 Back-of-book section: Abbr.
83 Private eye
84 Sailor's patron saint
86 Calliope's sister
88 '30s actress Velez
90 Magnavox rival
92 Bad impression?
94 Gaucho's weapon

96 NASA rocket stage
98 Conductor Seiji
100 Clear __
103 Raise, as crops
104 Boston's airport
105 Sleeveless cloak
106 Compass pt.
107 Whitish shade
108 Store-window sign

DOWN

1 "Blame It on the __ Nova"
2 __ Dhabi
3 Coal product
4 Wild guess

5 Mosey
6 With, *The*, Redford film of '88
7 Swimsuit part
8 "__ date!"
9 Emlyn Williams play
10 Actress Thurman
11 Tough to solve
12 Jessica Tandy film of '91
13 Part of CPA
14 Red Skelton character
15 Popular rock group
18 Toy craze of the '80s
22 Not as fresh

25 Hole in your shoe
27 "Xanadu" singers
30 River deposit
31 Pique
33 Ford from Michigan
35 "__ lurks in the grass": Virgil
37 Roman censor
39 007 film producer
41 Tropical tree
47 "__ a Nightingale"
53 *Message from Nam* novelist
58 Legalese adverb
59 Family-room favorite
61 Make a comparison
64 Get the news
65 __ as (when)
67 Western Indian
68 Occult doctrine
71 Olympian matchmaker
79 German article
85 Big name in union history
87 Activist Hoffman
89 Son of Seth
91 Sea of __ (Black Sea arm)
93 A little night music
95 Ginger __
97 Impress mightily
99 In the past
101 Where the buoys are
102 100%

8

surnaming

by a. j. santora

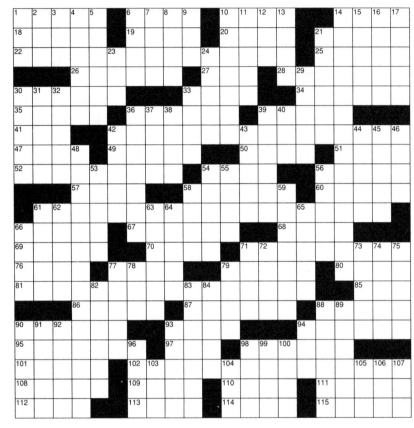

ACROSS
1 Apt initial answer
6 Laura of *Jurassic Park*
10 Egyptian slitherers
14 Bartlett relative
18 "With this ring __ wed"
19 Essayist's alias
20 Bouquet
21 __ Kinte (*Roots* role)
22 Fun-loving sort?
25 Later on
26 Dining area
27 Kauai side dish
28 The cost of leaving
30 2000 Summer Olympics city
33 Journalist Whitelaw
34 Jumped over
35 Full of the latest
36 Aft
39 Catch holder
41 "Botch-__" (Clooney tune)
42 Morning-after cocktail?
47 Livestock's lunch
49 Prevented squeaking
50 Brewer's oven
51 Powerful authority
52 Awaiting passengers
54 Toto's creator
56 Alda and Arkin
57 Forearm bone
58 Spanish, but not Canadian
60 Sad song
61 Made an imprudent exchange?
66 Al __ (pasta phrase)
67 Trenchermen
68 When summer leaves: Abbr.
69 Actor Davis

70 __-dansants (tea dances: Fr.)
71 Idaho sprout
76 MTV watcher
77 Gallic girlfriend
79 Mailroom stamp
80 Informal refusal
81 Broadway groupies?
85 Ghost-chance link
86 French spa
87 Let up
88 __ Lescaut (Puccini opera)
90 Head wreath of yore
93 Touched down
94 People under beds
95 *A Few Good Men* group

97 Treat with color
98 Somewhat risqué
101 That is, for long
102 Musical toy?
108 Barcelona boys
109 Olympian warmonger
110 Longfellow town
111 Sheikdom of song
112 *The Plague* setting
113 Numbers game
114 Shipshape
115 Javier __ de Cuellar

DOWN
1 Worthless trifle

2 "How was __ know?"
3 Greek letter
4 Family cars
5 Lipton competitor
6 Floor model
7 Alt.
8 University in Houston
9 See 80 Across
10 Furnish, as a dwelling
11 Well-founded
12 Pressure unit: Abbr.
13 In __ (harmonized)
14 Wild West star?
15 Ready to use
16 Metric area measure
17 Looked after, with "for"

21 Basketball Hall of Fame name
23 Gelid
24 Silly trick
29 Military state
30 Awful mess
31 Arab League charter member
32 High-school misfit
33 Comic Foxx
36 Surveyor's instrument
37 Fish dish
38 __ the mark (behaved)
39 Refuse to talk
40 Scale notes
42 Carried
43 "__ to My Head" ('38 tune)
44 Missouri range
45 __ bell (was familiar)
46 Scots Gaelic
48 Skeptic?

53 *Seascape* playwright
54 Mannerless sorts
55 Tiny colonists
56 Roll with the punches
58 Locust, for one
59 London district
61 Bowling button
62 Southend-__ (Thames resort)
63 Republic, e.g.
64 Clear sky
65 A dog's age
66 They may be connected
71 Gone by
72 Bison hunters
73 *Have Gun, Will Travel* star
74 __ a promotion (being considered)
75 Senior members
77 __ a dozen (common)
78 Erstwhile New Zealand bird
79 W.C. Fields oath
82 What's happening
83 Cousteau's craft
84 __ *Irish Rose*
88 Bit of bad luck
89 Hold fast
90 Organic acid
91 Rock bottom
92 Sports palace
93 Jingle writers
94 Smash
96 Badlands Natl. Park site
98 Computer-storage measure
99 Modena money
100 Troop group
103 Two-way preposition
104 Caesar follower
105 Chocolate shape
106 Brit. decoration
107 Apt final answer

trip payne

Professional crossword creator. Home: Georgia

Previous Occupation
Editor of three crossword magazines.

Education
B.A. in English from Emory University.

Crossword Credentials
Member of first-place United States team at the International Crossword Marathon (1990). Youngest winner of the American Crossword Puzzle Tournament (1993). Co-creator of the Sunday crossword distributed by United Feature Syndicate. Contributing editor and regular contributor to *Games* magazine. His puzzles appear regularly in *The New York Times*, the Uptown Puzzle Club, *Tough Cryptics*, *The Best of TV Guide Crosswords* magazine, and *Amtrak* magazine.

At age 25, Trip is the youngest contributor to *Masterpiece*, but he already has a decade of puzzlemaking experience under his belt. My professional relationship with him began on a humorous note. Seeing a distinctive talent in some of his early published puzzles, I tracked down Trip's phone number. My first call reached Mrs. Payne, who told me that Trip wasn't in – "He's in school now." I asked if he was a teacher, and she replied, "No, he's a high school student!"

The objective at the International Crossword Marathon, formerly held annually in various Eastern European locations, was to create the largest possible crossword in 24 consecutive hours. Teams representing each country consisted of four constructors and a captain/referee, who ensured that the team's crossword followed that country's puzzlemaking rules. To prevent a team from bringing a previously made crossword, the host country provided a set of words that had to be placed in a particular column (chosen at random as the event began).

The 1990 Marathon, held in Bjelovar, Yugoslavia, saw a new world's record established. The U.S. team, which included Trip, captured first place by creating a crossword over 160 feet long!

Puzzle #9 - "Who's Jean-Luc?"
An one-of-a-kind theme, perhaps the only three famous people with this particular first name. Note that the theme answers have unusual lengths for a 15x15 – two 14's and a 13. This necessitates an unusual diagram, with 16 of the Down answers having six or more letters.

Puzzle #10 - "By Any Measure"
The three brand names in this puzzle remind me of the so-called controversy associated with their inclusion in contemporary crosswords. One oldtime editor has been quoted as saying, "It smacks of PR." My response to that – 14 Down! Brand names are an integral part of our popular culture, and they have been seen in puzzles since the 1950s, when Margaret Farrar began to use them in *The New York Times*.

Puzzle #11 - "Face the Music"
One of the tougher puzzles in the book, with a host of new definitions for common words. There's also a lot of wordplay in the nontheme answers – sometimes signaled by a question mark, sometimes not.

Puzzle #12 - "Alphabetical Order"
Another unusual theme, executed in alphabetical order! Fortunately, Trip ran out of room before having to deal with GH. Many interesting nontheme clues (the result of extra digging), such as 53 Across, 60 Across, 1 Down, and 35 Down.

9
who's jean-luc?
by trip payne

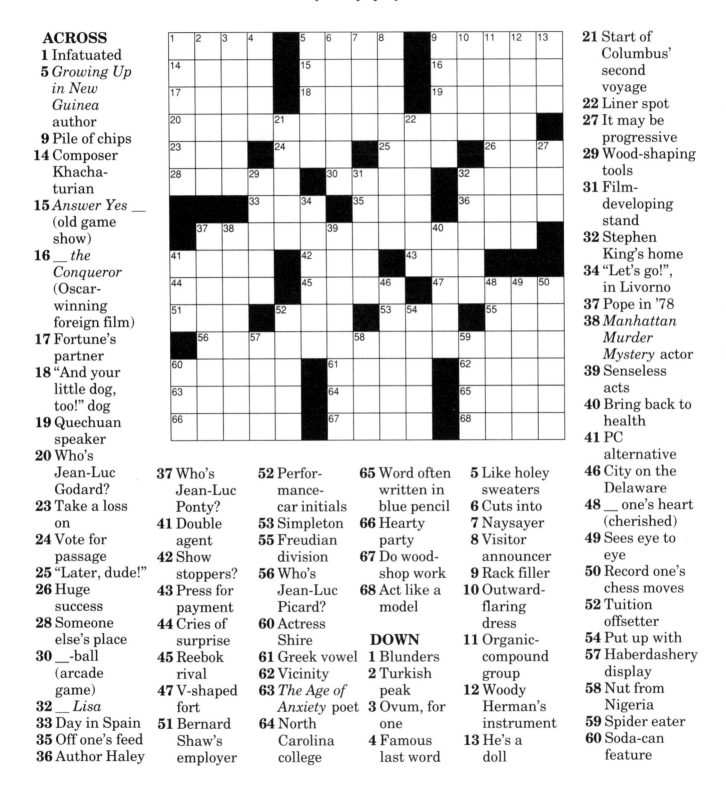

ACROSS
1 Infatuated
5 *Growing Up in New Guinea* author
9 Pile of chips
14 Composer Khacha- turian
15 *Answer Yes __* (old game show)
16 __ *the Conqueror* (Oscar- winning foreign film)
17 Fortune's partner
18 "And your little dog, too!" dog
19 Quechuan speaker
20 Who's Jean-Luc Godard?
23 Take a loss on
24 Vote for passage
25 "Later, dude!"
26 Huge success
28 Someone else's place
30 __-ball (arcade game)
32 __ *Lisa*
33 Day in Spain
35 Off one's feed
36 Author Haley

37 Who's Jean-Luc Ponty?
41 Double agent
42 Show stoppers?
43 Press for payment
44 Cries of surprise
45 Reebok rival
47 V-shaped fort
51 Bernard Shaw's employer

52 Perfor- mance- car initials
53 Simpleton
55 Freudian division
56 Who's Jean-Luc Picard?
60 Actress Shire
61 Greek vowel
62 Vicinity
63 *The Age of Anxiety* poet
64 North Carolina college

65 Word often written in blue pencil
66 Hearty party
67 Do wood- shop work
68 Act like a model

DOWN
1 Blunders
2 Turkish peak
3 Ovum, for one
4 Famous last word

5 Like holey sweaters
6 Cuts into
7 Naysayer
8 Visitor announcer
9 Rack filler
10 Outward- flaring dress
11 Organic- compound group
12 Woody Herman's instrument
13 He's a doll

21 Start of Columbus' second voyage
22 Liner spot
27 It may be progressive
29 Wood-shaping tools
31 Film- developing stand
32 Stephen King's home
34 "Let's go!", in Livorno
37 Pope in '78
38 *Manhattan Murder Mystery* actor
39 Senseless acts
40 Bring back to health
41 PC alternative
46 City on the Delaware
48 __ one's heart (cherished)
49 Sees eye to eye
50 Record one's chess moves
52 Tuition offsetter
54 Put up with
57 Haberdashery display
58 Nut from Nigeria
59 Spider eater
60 Soda-can feature

10

by any measure

by trip payne

ACROSS

1 Hockey player
7 Oust an attorney
13 Big-bang material
16 "I'd __ teach the world to sing . . ."
17 Loafer part
18 Anonymous Richard
19 Bolt-length units?
21 Country lodging
22 Discernment
23 *Goodness Had Nothing to Do With It* author
25 *I Remember __*
28 Pang
31 Life of Riley
32 Hail, to Horace
33 Curly smacker
34 Wood-weight units?
38 Mail again
40 Run counter to
41 Walrus feature
42 Racing Hall-of-Famer Breedlove
43 Coal holder
44 Long March leader
46 Mystery writer Josephine
47 Cathedral-length units?
51 Speedometer abbr.
54 Give it a whirl
55 Feedbag bit
56 John Wayne, by birth
60 Commodore Perry's headquarters
62 It's a fact

64 Imported auto
65 Weimaraner-weight units?
67 Dream-activity acronym
68 Family reuners
69 What you used to be?
70 Convoy members, often
72 *Blind Ambition* author
73 Face Hulk Hogan
76 Preposterous
78 Sculler's implement

79 Car-lot length units?
85 Old French coin
86 Take off one's boots
87 Former New Hampshire capital
88 "The racer's edge"
89 Move unsteadily
90 Leaves the flock

DOWN
1 Under the weather
2 XVII x VI
3 Heart chart

4 Conductor from Bombay
5 "__ way to go!"
6 Like fast flights
7 Hash house
8 "Minuet __"
9 Kazakhstan, formerly: Abbr.
10 Rapid growth
11 Hawkeye Pierce portrayer
12 Look for again
13 Competes for a part

14 Baloney
15 Caterpillar's structure
20 __ *Jury* (Spillane book)
24 Word on a bulb
25 Mr. Chagall
26 State assuredly
27 Phoenix suburb
29 Real-estate event
30 Right-angle shape
33 Bodily strength
35 Strive for
36 In the vicinity

37 Word with light or write
39 Sot's sound
40 Write Bros. rival
43 "Cross of Gold" orator
45 State of infamy
48 Official language of Pakistan
49 Verb for Popeye
50 Whimper
51 Pre-__ student
52 Draw out
53 Superior officer
57 Water-skier's path
58 Recitative's relative
59 Senator Sam
61 Heroic poetry
63 Football scoring plays, for short
64 Tropical trees
66 Computer reports, e.g.
67 Encircle
71 Grumpy and Dopey's occupation
72 Turn aside
73 Calamities
74 Freeway section
75 Agatha's colleague
77 Barber's cry
80 *Krazy __*
81 Top tortes
82 H as in Hellenic
83 Actor Alejandro
84 Grads-to-be: Abbr.

11

face the music

by trip payne

ACROSS

1 Rio dance
6 Basketball stadium
11 Grass-eating jumper
17 UFO pilot
18 Writer Runyon
19 Gym shoe
20 United Nations music?
22 Catherine or Alexandra
23 "Don't take this out"
24 Impressionist
25 Hilarious person
27 Drawer attachment
28 Journal notation
29 Fouled up
31 Medium-sized wildcats
35 It features "Please Mr. Postman"?
40 Some thrushes
41 Make happy
43 Not a soul
44 Rake over the __
45 "Lemon Tree" singer Lopez
46 Speedboat competition
48 Freud's daughter
49 Smith Brother feature
50 Disraeli's title
51 Extremely popular
52 Feta '45s?
56 Sam Spade, e.g.
59 Author Sarah __ Jewett
60 "We're Off __ the Wizard"
61 Item that makes one lightheaded?
65 Anagram for "regally"

67 Baseball great Wagner
68 Put in a box
69 Oscar-winner Davis
70 Grant recipient
71 Like some peanuts
72 Rendition of "Roamin' in the Gloamin' "?
75 Fast flashes
76 Spooky
77 Easily-caught fly
79 Couscous ingredients
83 Negative suffix
84 Post-deuce situation
85 Young lady
89 Never surpassed

91 "Leaving on a Jet Plane" genre?
94 Splits apart
95 Sheepish?
96 __-ease (uncomfortable)
97 Untold story
98 Olympic symbol
99 Intersects

DOWN

1 Hackneyed sayings
2 Like crazy
3 Stick in the mud
4 Part of Batman's uniform
5 What a comma may mean

6 Well-trained ones
7 10 Down, for example
8 Atlanta university
9 Lillehammer's land: Abbr.
10 Indy 500 winner Mario
11 Marching correctly
12 "Oh, give __ home . . ."
13 Gearshift selection
14 In the same category
15 Late-night TV name
16 Riyadh resident
19 Act angrily
21 Acts angrily

26 *"Dies __"*
28 Zillions of years
30 Use a participle without a subject
31 Willy, in *Free Willy*
32 __ dog (hunting hound)
33 Israeli statesman
34 One of Whitman's bloomers
35 Sedimentary rock
36 Mauna __
37 This and that
38 "A lamp __ my feet"
39 Chops, for example

41 Wipe clean
42 Italian bread?
45 Minuscule
46 Is in tumult
47 Perry's creator
49 Hazard to navigation
50 Take place next
53 *Ars Poetica* poet
54 Actress Skye
55 Lithified mud
56 License plates
57 TVA concern
58 Jazz singer Laine
62 Nora's pet
63 Onion relative
64 Mathematical chances
66 Medical specialty, for short
67 Makes a wish
68 Gefilte-fish ingredient
70 Speaker's place
71 Overcharged
73 Motorcycle-law subject
74 Leaves' home
75 Succulents' stickers
77 Contribute
78 Experiencing excessively
79 Congressional contributors
80 *Mirabella* rival
81 One of the Baldwin brothers
82 Film-rating unit
85 Race distance
86 Land in the water?
87 "Get lost!"
88 Mach 2 fliers
90 "__ been had!"
92 XIV x IV
93 Turn down the wattage

12
alphabetical order
by trip payne

ACROSS
1 Put on board
5 Honey bunch
9 Big fusses
13 Fun's partner
18 Colleague of Dashiell and Agatha
19 Caesarean phrase
20 Magicians' birds
22 Mideasterner
23 Soft mineral
24 Letters on an envelope
25 Water or wine
26 Peripheral
27 AB
31 Do the hula
32 Nonstandard negative
33 Like some cakes
37 From __ Z
38 Sporty-car initials
39 Old Testament villain
42 Actor Wallach
43 Take __ (suffer losses)
46 *B.C.*
50 Walk-on role
51 "You __ Beautiful" ('75 tune)
52 Mork's home planet
53 __ Richelieu (Paris street)
54 "__ was saying . . ."
55 Short skirts
57 Be inconsistent
59 Added up
60 Baryshnikov's birthplace
62 '20s auto
63 TV rooms
64 Kind of vaccine
65 CD
71 Reasons not to
72 Slugger's rewards
73 Venerable
74 Wall features?

76 Mutated gene
79 Reasons to
80 Messy places
82 "Can't Help Lovin' __ Man"
83 Virtuous one
84 Cousteau's realm
85 Cronos or Rhea
87 Come together
89 DE
92 Plains Indians' prey
93 WWII arena
94 Musical tempo
95 *Wheel of Fortune* purchase
96 Sallow-faced
97 Arcade favorite
100 Fuse metal

102 Soft touch
105 E.F.
110 *Chicago Sun-Times* reviewer
113 __ Bell (a Brontë pseudonym)
114 Other things: Lat.
115 __ *kleine Nachtmusik*
116 They may be common
117 Newscaster Sawyer
118 Norwegian name
119 Western actor Jack
120 Dictatorial
121 Work units
122 Ocean motion
123 Caligula's nephew

DOWN
1 Character in *The Iliad*
2 Gorilla kin
3 Cat's hangout
4 Festoon
5 __ the punch (do first)
6 __ *Extra-Terrestrial*
7 Major ending
8 Catches some rays
9 Annex
10 Skater Hamill
11 *Metamorphoses* poet
12 Faxed, perhaps
13 Like tollhouse cookies
14 Tickle one's fancy
15 Wrestler's surface
16 Chemical ending

17 Polite address
21 Shelley's "blithe spirit"
28 About 1.8 meters
29 Literary celebs
30 Breathe heavily
34 Convened again
35 Say "vow'l," for example
36 Chopped finely
38 Balzac's *Le Pere __*
40 Richard's cry
41 "A grand old name"
43 Hertz Rent-__
44 Elementary
45 Guatemalan girlfriend
46 Blair and Leigh
47 Queen and King, for two
48 Dubrovnik resident
49 Extend

56 Vernon Castle's dancing partner
58 Farm animals
59 Big-league deal
61 Work one's way up
63 Olivia of *The Wonder Years*
64 Operating, as a computer
66 Maestro from Hungary
67 Moving aimlessly
68 Take turns
69 *Quo __?*
70 Love-poetry Muse
75 British carbine
76 Take __ in the right direction
77 Actress Christine
78 Be supported by
79 Unskilled laborer
80 Refuse to move
81 Imported auto
84 Processed ore
86 Author Calvino
88 Old enough to vote last year
90 "___ Ever Need Is You"
91 *Father __ Mysteries*
96 Waikiki woman
98 Badminton needs
99 Prone to fidgeting
101 Slalom curves
102 Proclaimed publicly
103 Subway entrance
104 Destroyer device
106 Nastase of tennis
107 Winglike
108 264 qvadrvpled?
109 James Mason role
110 Flow back
111 *To Kill a Mockingbird* hermit
112 Dash lengths

mel rosen

Crossword editor, constructor, author, and software developer. Home: Florida

Previous Occupation
Computer analyst.

Education
Attended the University of Chicago and Vassar College.

Crossword Credentials
New York Times contributor since 1970. Editor of 44 crossword collections in book form since 1983. Coauthor of *The Compleat Cruciverbalist – How to Solve, Compose, and Sell Crossword Puzzles*. Succeeded Will Weng as editor for The Crosswords Club in 1993.

Mel Rosen's unique "middle-of-the-road" style defies the standard categorization of crosswords, which are usually classified as "traditional" or "contemporary." This may be due to his age – between that of the baby boom "new wavers" and the sixtysomething traditionalists. More likely, Mel has simply found qualities worth emulating from each group.

Mel credits his mother, a retired teacher specializing in reading skills, with giving him an appreciation of words long before he knew anything about puzzles. His first published puzzle, created with his wife Peggy, wasn't a crossword. It was an acrostic, which appeared in a Tom Middleton book published over 20 years ago.

A former employee of IBM, Mel was a pioneer in the use of personal computers in the puzzle business. His software program CWP™, which automates crossword editorial functions, is used today by many puzzle professionals. Also, he was the first to devise a PC-based typesetting system for crosswords, first used for a tournament he directed in 1987.

Puzzle #13 - "Sound Effects"
Mel is an uproariously funny fellow in person, famous in puzzle circles for his quick, sharp wit. His theme for this puzzle reflects his "sound" sense of humor.

Puzzle #14 - "Collectibles"
The rules followed by puzzle creators and editors today were developed by Margaret Farrar, first crossword editor of *The New York Times* and puzzledom's most revered figure. These rules include diagram symmetry, maximum number of answers in various puzzle sizes, and so on. It's not often that the rules are relaxed, but when they are, there's a good reason. It won't reveal too much to tell you that the theme of this puzzle involves the breaking of one of the standard editorial rules.

Puzzle #15 - "Lesser-Known Associates"
Another humorous theme. This time, a skewed look at some famous people of fact and fiction.

Puzzle #16 - "Tom Swifties Revisited"
Tom Swifties are a time-honored form of wordplay. If you're not familiar with them, you might miss the relationship between the clues and the answers at first glance. Take a good look at the operative word in each theme clue, and it should all become clear.

13
sound effects
by mel rosen

ACROSS
1 Drive the getaway car, perhaps
5 '20s avant-garde art movement
9 Twists out of shape
14 Lomond, for one
15 *A Summer Place* star
16 "__ a Symphony" (Supremes song)
17 Low-quality
18 Immunological agents
19 Dizzy and Jimmy
20 Lamb's lament?
23 Miscalculates
24 Split apart
25 Sheep's cheer?
29 Where to see Larry King
32 Rich, as foods
33 Plate cleaner
34 Ballet bend
35 Felipe's female friend
36 Air-gun ammo

37 Quench
38 Declares illegal
39 Heavenly body
40 Parted with
41 Compass pt.
42 Barnyard singer?
44 "The __ Love"
46 "*Vesti la giubba*" is one
47 Asinine insect?

52 __ de Lion (Richard I)
53 Ostentation
54 Pastoral poem
56 Kicking's partner
57 Lotion additive
58 Forbidden thing
59 *Star Trek* doctor's nickname
60 Namesakes of a Bobbsey

61 __ plaid (fabric pattern)

DOWN
1 Height of a European vacation?
2 Ninny
3 Greenpeace's concern: Abbr.
4 Wool complement of rhyme
5 Wipe out

6 AARP's anathema
7 "Rats!"
8 Word-forming game
9 Improve a freeway
10 Coming up
11 Stern
12 Breathe hard
13 Alums-to-be: Abbr.
21 Luncheonette lure
22 Bucket of bolts

25 Strikebreakers
26 La Douce et al.
27 View from the Left Bank
28 Good ol' boy
29 One of California's Santas
30 Court wear
31 Calls for
34 Acting conciliatory
36 Cranium
37 '92 Summer Olympics host
39 Science magazine
40 Spanish shawls
43 Wealth personified
44 Pale purple
45 Filmdom's Dr. Kildare
47 Machete's cousin
48 Harness attachment
49 NBA Hall-of-Famer Tom
50 Object of adulation
51 Last word of a 1/1 tune
52 Truck compartment
55 Nol of Cambodia

14
collectibles
by mel rosen

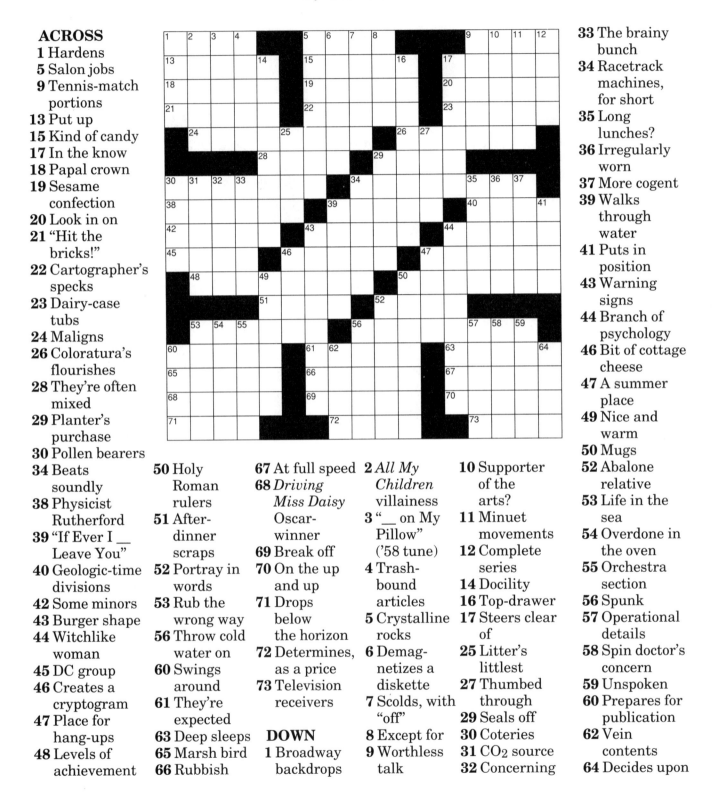

ACROSS

1 Hardens
5 Salon jobs
9 Tennis-match portions
13 Put up
15 Kind of candy
17 In the know
18 Papal crown
19 Sesame confection
20 Look in on
21 "Hit the bricks!"
22 Cartographer's specks
23 Dairy-case tubs
24 Maligns
26 Coloratura's flourishes
28 They're often mixed
29 Planter's purchase
30 Pollen bearers
34 Beats soundly
38 Physicist Rutherford
39 "If Ever I __ Leave You"
40 Geologic-time divisions
42 Some minors
43 Burger shape
44 Witchlike woman
45 DC group
46 Creates a cryptogram
47 Place for hang-ups
48 Levels of achievement

50 Holy Roman rulers
51 After-dinner scraps
52 Portray in words
53 Rub the wrong way
56 Throw cold water on
60 Swings around
61 They're expected
63 Deep sleeps
65 Marsh bird
66 Rubbish

67 At full speed
68 *Driving Miss Daisy* Oscar-winner
69 Break off
70 On the up and up
71 Drops below the horizon
72 Determines, as a price
73 Television receivers

DOWN
1 Broadway backdrops

2 *All My Children* villainess
3 "__ on My Pillow" ('58 tune)
4 Trash-bound articles
5 Crystalline rocks
6 Demag-netizes a diskette
7 Scolds, with "off"
8 Except for
9 Worthless talk

10 Supporter of the arts?
11 Minuet movements
12 Complete series
14 Docility
16 Top-drawer
17 Steers clear of
25 Litter's littlest
27 Thumbed through
29 Seals off
30 Coteries
31 CO_2 source
32 Concerning

33 The brainy bunch
34 Racetrack machines, for short
35 Long lunches?
36 Irregularly worn
37 More cogent
39 Walks through water
41 Puts in position
43 Warning signs
44 Branch of psychology
46 Bit of cottage cheese
47 A summer place
49 Nice and warm
50 Mugs
52 Abalone relative
53 Life in the sea
54 Overdone in the oven
55 Orchestra section
56 Spunk
57 Operational details
58 Spin doctor's concern
59 Unspoken
60 Prepares for publication
62 Vein contents
64 Decides upon

15

lesser-known associates

by mel rosen

ACROSS

1 Subjective sensations
6 Shaving-cream type
9 Past curfew
13 Pedestal part
17 Prepared to be knighted
18 Ga. neighbor
19 Actress Chase
20 Isaac's eldest
21 Joan of Arc's associate?
25 Fitness center
26 Yul's *Solomon and Sheba* costar
27 Cam-valve connector
28 Hit hard
31 Spec record
32 Sigher's phrase
33 Rosinante?
39 Feel off
40 Ornamental mat
41 401(k) cousins
42 Picnic entree
43 Weevil's lunch
45 Start of the 16th century
46 Port in a storm
48 *Mr. Hulot's Holiday* director/star
49 History chapters, perhaps
51 Sugar suffix
52 Special Forces wear
53 George Washington's sister?
60 Longwinded
61 TV's 14 through 83
62 K-P filler
63 Electrolysis participants
64 Tiny bits

66 Grain-storage place
67 Slangy denial
71 Part of MS
72 Fly in the ointment
73 Having two lobes
75 Spring time
76 Antonio's client?
81 Hawaiian cookie tycoon
82 Messenger goddess
83 Held the floor
84 Memory trace
87 Prof.'s rank
88 Slow down, in mus.
89 Figaro's concessionaire?
96 "This __ outrage!"

97 Give up
98 '90s informal exclamation
99 Lake Geneva resort
100 Pro follower
101 Did some cultivation
102 Smiley's occupation
103 Exploits

DOWN

1 Police-blotter abbr.
2 Burma's first prime minister
3 Sales agent, for short
4 Michener novel
5 Scholarship allowance

6 Zinger, for instance
7 Bush was one in the '40s
8 For the most part
9 The __ Judah (Haile Selassie)
10 __ Romeo (imported auto)
11 WBC result
12 Sci-fi being
13 Become more intense
14 Rush-order letters
15 Isak Dinesen, by birth
16 Depose
22 Sparks' job on ship
23 Wheels of fortune?

24 Esther Williams' ex
28 Shot in the dark
29 Louisville's river
30 Honeycomb unit
31 Flamboyant surrealist
32 Berne's river
34 Central point
35 Pâté base
36 Technical analyst's creation
37 Misanthrope
38 Town terrorized in *Jaws*
44 Sales prospects
46 Dances like Ann Miller
47 Tempe sch.
48 Mortise insert

50 __ Lopez (early chess analyst)
52 Dinner roll
53 Dance along with Chubby
54 Bootleg booze
55 Bert's *Sesame Street* pal
56 Expenses
57 Mtge.-insurance agcy.
58 Hanger's place?
59 Opossum, for example
64 To such a degree
65 Dinner for Dobbin
66 Life stories
68 Skip past
69 Harness race
70 Beheld
72 Cashew-family tree
73 Liverpudlians and Cantabrigians
74 Proved a theorem
77 Constellation within Argo
78 Overlooked
79 Formerly, old-style
80 Sabra, vis-à-vis Israel
84 Mideast ruler
85 Skylab launcher
86 Small fly
87 Army adjutant, e.g.
90 '20s auto
91 Popinjay
92 Unkempt quarters
93 Don't play it straight
94 Schoolboy
95 Recent USNA graduate

16

tom swifties revisited

by mel rosen

ACROSS

1 Strong acid, to a chemist
4 Shaft adjunct
7 Keep up with the times
12 Short to-dos
17 London nitery district
18 Latin 101 verb
19 Pacific Coast Highway town
21 Attacked
22 "__," said Tom, forgivingly
26 Cannes vista
27 Release
28 Marseille menu
29 Genealogy diagram
30 Praiseworthy
32 Thrifty sort
35 Relaxes
37 Bed of roses
38 Art __
39 R.E. Lee org.
40 "__," said Tom, overbearingly
50 Pre-med course: Abbr.
51 Recess activity
52 Whirlpool product
53 Tap trouble
54 Million-byte units, in computerese
55 Mrs. Munster
56 Scoundrel
57 Extravagantly theatrical
58 Interdict
59 Greek cross
60 Get __ of (notice)
61 React to fireworks, perhaps
62 "__," said Tom, proverbially
70 GPs' org.
71 Walking with a sprained ankle
72 Marciano's pride
73 Dig in
74 Rump-roast rating
77 Kathie Lee's cohost
78 European industrial region
80 Actress __ May Wong
81 Icicle holder
82 Sci-fi weapon
83 Sissy
84 Part of a bridal outfit
85 "__," said Tom, implicitly
90 Comic Kabibble
91 Objectives
92 Leander's love
93 Adverb in a contract
97 Rich cake
99 Dined sumptuously
102 Holiday season
103 Victorian novelist . . .
105 . . . and one of her characters
107 "What'll __?" (Berlin song)
108 "__," said Tom, constrainedly
113 Flowed slowly
114 Leave the Union
115 Hearth leftovers
116 LAX postings
117 Mosquito relatives
118 Venturesome one
119 "__ Loves You" (early Beatles tune)
120 Eur. language

DOWN

1 Old Testament book
2 Holy Roman Empire founder
3 Colleague of Boris and Bela
4 Blondie's occupation
5 Friendship
6 Synthesizer name
7 Volume-boosting equipment
8 "Zip-A-Dee-Doo-__"
9 *Love, __* (Audrey Meadows book)
10 *For Whom the Bell Tolls* character
11 Ski-resort transit
12 Librarian's warning
13 *Henry VI, __*
14 Festoon
15 Patched up, in a way
16 Eye irritations
17 Featherbrain
20 Not securely in bed, maybe
23 Lock horns
24 Bouquet
25 Stretching muscle
31 Helm and Dillon
33 "__ Breaky Heart" (Billy Ray Cyrus tune)
34 Take a pledge
36 Mouthful of gum
38 In need of sharpening
40 Metrical feet
41 Keep __ to the ground
42 Perfume brand
43 Senseless behavior
44 Delightful experience
45 Fourth most widely spoken language
46 Home of the Nez Percé Indians
47 Hand holder
48 Kenyan track star Keino
49 Fifth columnist
55 Asian monk
56 Book-jacket parts
57 *Far Side* regulars
59 "Sock it __!"
60 Look up to
61 __ about close to schedule
63 Military-school student
64 Cast off, biologically
65 British actor Bruce
66 Congo cud-chewer
67 Work towards a new contract
68 City near Miami
69 Play for time
74 Catch on to
75 Show team spirit
76 Bogie's costar in *The Barefoot Contessa*
77 Unenviable quarters
78 "Chocolate point" cat
79 Qtys.
80 States confidently
82 First word of a Longfellow poem
83 Habeas corpus, e.g.
86 Pinocchio's undoing
87 The 19th hole
88 Put away, as a sword
89 Car-purchase alternative
93 Desktop-publishing skill, for short
94 Port __, MI
95 Alfred P. Doolittle's daughter
96 Stopwatch button
97 Puccini's opera singer
98 Additional
99 Five diamonds, in Vegas
100 Moonwalking astronaut Mitchell
101 Accomplishes
104 Teed off
106 "Take __ a compliment!"
109 Army uniforms, for short
110 Summer cooler
111 Part of KJV
112 Journey part

donna j. stone

Professional crossword creator. Home: New Jersey

Previous Occupation
High-school Latin teacher.

Education
B.A. in classical languages from St. Peter's College (Jersey City, NJ).

Crossword Credentials
Sold first crossword in 1983. Creator of a nationally syndicated Sunday crossword. Creator of the weekly TV crossword for *New York Newsday*. Regular contributor to the *Newsday* daily crossword, the Uptown Puzzle Club, and numerous puzzle magazines.

Unique among puzzlemakers, Donna has never been a regular solver of crosswords. Her career started when she bought a puzzle magazine to pass the time, and found herself curious about how puzzles were created. She then learned the craft by tracking down every available book on puzzlemaking.

Donna is best known for her quotation puzzles – in particular, her *funny* quotation puzzles. She hit upon her specialty after noticing the quotations used in puzzles at that time all seemed to be serious and erudite, by authors like Jefferson and Gandhi. As a result, her puzzles require much more preparation than usual, since usable quotes must be divisible into symmetric parts as well as funny.

Other features you can expect in a typical Donna Stone puzzle (all of which can be found in each of her *Masterpiece* puzzles): a clever title that incorporates the main idea of the quotation, generous helpings of wordplay in the clues, and (her trademark) the use of all 26 letters of the alphabet!

Puzzle #17 - "Lost Youth"
A one-liner from a comic who made numerous appearances on *The Ed Sullivan Show*. Note all the question marks in the clues – a sure sign that there's a whole lotta punnin' goin' on.

Puzzle #18 - "Aswan Calling!"
Not exactly a quote, the theme consists of an "age-old" riddle and an answer that may make you groan. Many interesting words and phrases are found in the nontheme answers – a direct result of all 26 letters being present.

Puzzle #19 - "Amen!"
A quote with both a religious and an educational flavor, which Donna obtained from the quotation magazine to which she subscribes.

Puzzle #20 - "On the Rocks"
A theme having nothing to do with ice or drinks.

17
lost youth
by donna j. stone

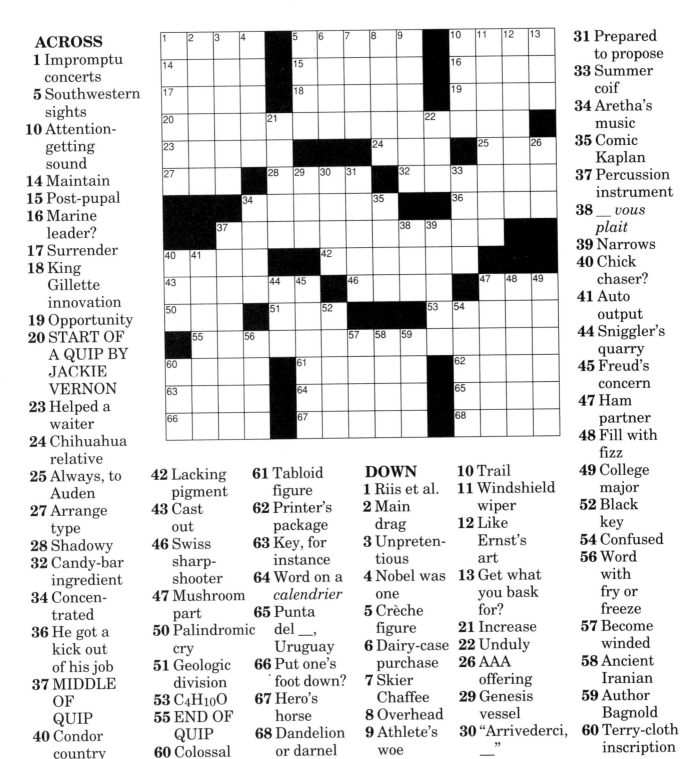

ACROSS

1 Impromptu concerts
5 Southwestern sights
10 Attention-getting sound
14 Maintain
15 Post-pupal
16 Marine leader?
17 Surrender
18 King Gillette innovation
19 Opportunity
20 START OF A QUIP BY JACKIE VERNON
23 Helped a waiter
24 Chihuahua relative
25 Always, to Auden
27 Arrange type
28 Shadowy
32 Candy-bar ingredient
34 Concentrated
36 He got a kick out of his job
37 MIDDLE OF QUIP
40 Condor country
42 Lacking pigment
43 Cast out
46 Swiss sharpshooter
47 Mushroom part
50 Palindromic cry
51 Geologic division
53 C₄H₁₀O
55 END OF QUIP
60 Colossal
61 Tabloid figure
62 Printer's package
63 Key, for instance
64 Word on a *calendrier*
65 Punta del __, Uruguay
66 Put one's foot down?
67 Hero's horse
68 Dandelion or darnel

DOWN

1 Riis et al.
2 Main drag
3 Unpretentious
4 Nobel was one
5 Crèche figure
6 Dairy-case purchase
7 Skier Chaffee
8 Overhead
9 Athlete's woe
10 Trail
11 Windshield wiper
12 Like Ernst's art
13 Get what you bask for?
21 Increase
22 Unduly
26 AAA offering
29 Genesis vessel
30 "Arrivederci, __"
31 Prepared to propose
33 Summer coif
34 Aretha's music
35 Comic Kaplan
37 Percussion instrument
38 __ *vous plait*
39 Narrows
40 Chick chaser?
41 Auto output
44 Sniggler's quarry
45 Freud's concern
47 Ham partner
48 Fill with fizz
49 College major
52 Black key
54 Confused
56 Word with fry or freeze
57 Become winded
58 Ancient Iranian
59 Author Bagnold
60 Terry-cloth inscription

18
aswan calling!
by donna j. stone

ACROSS
1 Khan opener?
4 Grand __ Island
10 Remote
16 Hair ball?
17 Persephone's love
18 Swimmer in the news in '26
19 Kiddie __ (*Jeopardy!* category)
20 START OF A RIDDLE
22 *Idylls of the King* character
24 Singer Zadora
25 Soup scoop
26 Avenge
28 Leaves behind
32 Bee and Em
33 Grows faint
34 Colorado resort
35 Was careless with cream
36 __ *souci* (carefree)
37 Itty-bitty
39 Khrushchev colleague
40 Shatner role
41 Lobster __ Diavolo
42 PART 2 OF RIDDLE
44 PART 3 OF RIDDLE
49 Popular street name
50 Alluring
51 Jai __

52 Hadrian's predecessor
56 Karras or Haley
57 Donut topping
58 Bank deposit?
59 Tater
60 Meeting place
61 Pottery type
64 Ultimate car
66 Persian cat?
67 Some collectibles
68 __ for one's money

69 ANSWER TO RIDDLE
74 Jack or jenny
75 Mutinied
76 Forsyth's *The __ File*
77 St. Anthony's cross
78 Adapted
79 Decimal divisions
80 Compass pt.

DOWN
1 Less inept
2 Pet-shop purchase

3 The old days?
4 Grump's comment
5 Takes on
6 Comic Mandel
7 *Three Men __ Baby*
8 "*O Sole __*"
9 Sanctuaries
10 Clan clashes
11 Woman or mare
12 Self-restraint
13 Prospector's prize
14 Sanibel Isl.'s locale

15 Marsh
21 Mare's meal
23 Uniroyal rival
27 Addams Family cousin
28 Porker's proclamation
29 Smith of Rhodesia
30 Greek letters
31 Under-handed
33 Sew a toe
35 Canonized *Mlle.*

36 *The King and I* locale
37 Hector's home
38 Canal zone?
40 Potter's need
41 *Sanford and Son* star
43 Japanese export
44 Exploit
45 Panamanian money
46 Give details
47 Spinning server
48 Make up stories
50 Turn about
52 NFL stats.
53 Scoundrel
54 From __ Z
55 Literally "doorkeeper"
56 It may get into a jam
57 Dollop
59 Chopin's *cherie*
60 A trifle tardy
62 Get the lead out?
63 Tapered off
64 Cardinal feature
65 Happen next
67 Mass com-munication?
69 Yank
70 Uncover, in verse
71 Pray: Lat.
72 Pindaric poem
73 Ensign's base, perhaps: Abbr.

19
amen!
by donna j. stone

ACROSS

1 *M*A*S*H* vehicle
5 "I've been __!"
8 Part of Einstein's equation
12 Breakfast-buffet tray
17 Winglike
18 Compass pt.
19 Countertenor
20 Santa Anna battleground
21 Toronto team
23 Novelist Didion
24 Handbag part
25 START OF A QUIP BY LARRY MILLER
28 Like a Vermont village
31 Green land
32 How Friends say "you"
33 Multicolored cereal
34 Stowe novel
35 Book-jacket feature
36 Snake-charmer's crew
40 Doctrine
41 Frog kin
43 Surprise-ending master
46 Chop down
47 Where kids eat
49 Name on the range, perhaps
50 Shilly-shally
52 Legendary meanie
53 Coll. cadets
54 Lacking principles
55 PART 2 OF QUIP

59 PART 3 OF QUIP
61 Served the chowder
62 Inspect too closely?
64 Reinforce a raincoat
65 I.e., for long
66 Gravy ingredient
67 Letter getter?
71 Be indisposed
72 City sounds
74 Singer __ Elliot
75 Stirrup site
76 Poor grades
78 Superman nemesis Luthor

79 Like Hitchcock's curtain
81 Greek-salad need
82 Tattled
84 Pisa dough
85 Stanley Cup, e.g.
87 END OF QUIP
92 World book
93 Knock about
94 Wildly reckless one
98 Pointless
99 Egyptian mother goddess
100 Exploit
101 Do in
102 Winds up
103 Rapscallions
104 Frat letter

105 "Omigosh!"

DOWN

1 Riddick Bowe blow
2 Pipe-fitter's union?
3 It's in the Seine
4 Add up front
5 *Damn Yankees* tune
6 Novelist Seton
7 Napoleon, at times
8 Household head
9 Unattended
10 Forest father
11 Clementi composition
12 Moisten meat

13 Tennis great Gibson
14 Give a hoot
15 General Bradley
16 "Uh-uh"
22 Garfield's owner
26 Tell it like it isn't
27 Restaurateur Toots
28 Stick it in your ear
29 Air bear
30 Zeroes in
34 Propeller-head
35 Where subs sit
37 Puppeteer Lewis
38 Power a trike
39 Great
41 Fast-food entree

42 Went wrong
44 Wonderland resident
45 Men of Mocha
48 Quarters for drivers?
49 Castile's companion
51 I is one
54 '87 Peace Prize winner
55 Ancient epic
56 Dogpatch denizen
57 Astaire's sister
58 Tony timer
60 Violinist Mischa
63 Vigor
66 Artist Remington
68 Road Runner's remark
69 Solemn statement
70 Revealing photo?
73 Poorly
74 Respond to a joke
77 Maroon
80 Hosp. areas
81 Down-to-earth
83 Dromedary depots?
84 Furious
85 *My Cousin Vinny* Oscar-winner
86 *Palais* potentate
87 It may be jumped
88 Sight from Catania
89 Blueprint
90 Soprano Ponselle
91 Diner fare
95 *Arabian Nights* name
96 Use the remote
97 Examine

20
on the rocks
by donna j. stone

ACROSS

1 Transvaal resident
5 Largest dolphin
9 Like opposites
14 Melodious McEntire
18 Proficient
19 Please Pavlov?
20 Mrs. Kramden
21 The yoke's on them
22 START OF A QUIP BY HERM ALBRIGHT
26 Occasional athlete
27 Cleaner scent
28 Kitchen gadget
29 Trickle
30 Like raisins
32 Eating alcove
34 Gambler's quest
37 Pick up
38 Folding items
39 PART 2 OF QUIP
42 Letter closer
46 Early Japanese capital
47 Enthusiastic
48 '58 Pulitzer Prize winner
49 Be important
50 Eccentric one
53 Mr. Bulba
55 Eary creatures?
56 *Evita* role
57 Medicine-show offering
59 Gala
60 '40s game-show group
65 PART 3 OF QUIP
66 Ado Annie's home
68 Invisible
69 Gulch
72 Sculler's implement
73 Harmonica virtuoso Larry
74 Delayed
75 Becky Thatcher's creator

81 Penn or Connery
82 Bone-dry
83 Fertile Crescent figure
84 Actress Swenson
85 Role for Shirley
86 PART 4 OF QUIP
91 Proof of ownership
92 Miss America's tenure
93 Add new info
94 __ oneself (lie under oath)
98 NHLer
99 Rainbow goddess
100 He's out of this world
101 Kick in

102 Some foreign nouns
106 END OF QUIP
112 Phone abbr.
113 Say "*&%@#*!"
114 Mead need
115 Horse color
116 Nitti's nemesis
117 Bestseller in a bear market?
118 __ Blanc
119 Unmarried *Mme.*

DOWN

1 Bughouse
2 Bassoon relative
3 Ancient Asian kingdom
4 College official
5 Frigate deck
6 Milne creature
7 Machine part
8 Actress MacGraw
9 Unfazed by delays
10 Chan portrayer
11 Lo-cal
12 Wagnerian exclamation
13 Auto acronym
14 Comedienne O'Donnell
15 Precise
16 *The Devil and Daniel Webster* writer
17 Conductor Kostelanetz
19 Sounds of music?
23 Fencing blades
24 Richard's veep
25 Coffee brewers
30 Yearning
31 Durban dough

32 Kierkegaard and Bohr
33 *Picnic* playwright
34 Out of __ (incompatible)
35 "Right on!"
36 Poet Teasdale
37 Wash
38 Barber of Seville
40 Filled to the gills
41 Mata __
42 Audacious
43 Keep an __ the ground
44 Cook veggies
45 Alternating-current innovator
51 Field: Ger.
52 Vandyke site
53 Actress Meg or Jennifer
54 Ferris-wheel part
55 Bravery

58 Praise publicly
59 Bad press
60 Resembling
61 In a trance
62 Riyadh's religion
63 Mrs. Ethan Frome
64 Yellow
67 Hyundai's home
70 Utah city
71 Materialize
74 Snickering sound
76 Yemeni seaport
77 Shutter shaker
78 Author Sewell
79 "__ Plenty o' Nuttin'"
80 Thurmond of basketball
82 Trick ending
83 World leader portrayed by Ingrid Bergman
87 Eloquence
88 Dictator's defier
89 Collateral
90 Soporific substance
91 *Heartbreak House* character
94 South African novelist
95 Take the honey and run?
96 Miffs
97 Greetings for the villain
98 PGA Hall-of-Famer
99 Atlas feature
101 Made cheddar better
103 Organic compound
104 Authentic
105 Ago, to Burns
107 Summer hrs.
108 Wonderment
109 German physicist
110 Sticky stuff
111 Bed-and-breakfast, e.g.

dean niles

Self-employed commodities trader. Home: Illinois

Previous Occupations
Copy editor for the *Encyclopaedia Britannica*, clergyman, group therapist, law-office administrator.

Education
B.A. in English literature from the University of Chicago, Doctor of Ministry in pastoral care and counseling from Chicago Theological Seminary.

Crossword Credentials
First crossword accepted for publication by Mel Rosen in 1992. Creator of the crossword for *Mensa Bulletin* (the monthly member magazine of American Mensa, the high-IQ society). Regular contributor to *The New York Times*, the *Newsday* crossword, the Uptown Puzzle Club, and numerous puzzle magazines.

Dean is the relative newcomer to puzzlemaking among *Masterpiece* contributors, with only two years of experience to date. However, he is probably the most prolific constructor in the group. By his own admission, most of his spare time (after the commodities markets close each day) is spent creating crosswords. A longtime solver, Dean first became interested in constructing in 1990, and credits Mel Rosen with providing him with the guidance and encouragement that allowed his skills to develop.

Like many puzzlemakers, Dean creates the kind of crosswords he would like to solve himself – not too easy, with wide-ranging subject matter. This includes a sprinkling of unfamiliar but interesting answer words. As a result, you may find Dean's quartet of *Masterpiece* puzzles a bit tougher than the rest.

Puzzle #21 - "Book Review"
The less-frequently used letters show up more often than usual. You may not be familiar with 9 Across or 4 Down, but (as many solvers find) you're apt to notice them in your general reading after noting them here.

Puzzle #22 - "Leftovers"
A *Jeopardy!* category provided the inspiration for this puzzle, which takes its name in a different direction from the game show. 13 and 33 Down are lesser-known but nonetheless interesting words. The quote at 85 Across comes from a verse of "I Get a Kick Out of You."

Puzzle #23 - "Silly Songs"
Most of the "words" that make up the theme answers won't be found in your dictionary . . . or any other standard reference book, for that matter. The answer at 38 Across is also the title of Peter Ustinov's autobiography. 28 Down is the town nearest the Four Corners Monument, the only place in the United States where you can stand in four states at the same time.

Puzzle #24 - "Beau Jest"
The title fits the theme perfectly. Dean thought of it *before* he made the puzzle. So it should help to do what he did – consider what a puzzle with this title would be about. There's an uncommon but lovely word at 109 Across; it's from the Latin for "play."

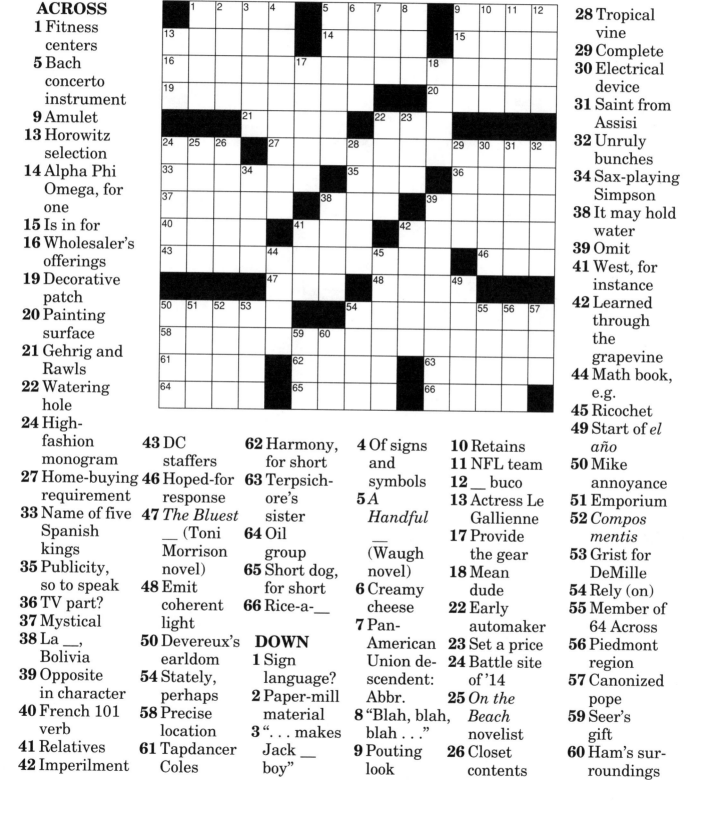

ACROSS

1 Fitness centers
5 Bach concerto instrument
9 Amulet
13 Horowitz selection
14 Alpha Phi Omega, for one
15 Is in for
16 Wholesaler's offerings
19 Decorative patch
20 Painting surface
21 Gehrig and Rawls
22 Watering hole
24 High-fashion monogram
27 Home-buying requirement
33 Name of five Spanish kings
35 Publicity, so to speak
36 TV part?
37 Mystical
38 La __, Bolivia
39 Opposite in character
40 French 101 verb
41 Relatives
42 Imperilment
43 DC staffers
46 Hoped-for response
47 *The Bluest __* (Toni Morrison novel)
48 Emit coherent light
50 Devereux's earldom
54 Stately, perhaps
58 Precise location
61 Tapdancer Coles
62 Harmony, for short
63 Terpsichore's sister
64 Oil group
65 Short dog, for short
66 Rice-a-__

DOWN

1 Sign language?
2 Paper-mill material
3 "... makes Jack __ boy"
4 Of signs and symbols
5 *A Handful __* (Waugh novel)
6 Creamy cheese
7 Pan-American Union descendent: Abbr.
8 "Blah, blah, blah ..."
9 Pouting look
10 Retains
11 NFL team
12 __ buco
13 Actress Le Gallienne
17 Provide the gear
18 Mean dude
22 Early automaker
23 Set a price
24 Battle site of '14
25 *On the Beach* novelist
26 Closet contents
28 Tropical vine
29 Complete
30 Electrical device
31 Saint from Assisi
32 Unruly bunches
34 Sax-playing Simpson
38 It may hold water
39 Omit
41 West, for instance
42 Learned through the grapevine
44 Math book, e.g.
45 Ricochet
49 Start of *el año*
50 Mike annoyance
51 Emporium
52 *Compos mentis*
53 Grist for DeMille
54 Rely (on)
55 Member of 64 Across
56 Piedmont region
57 Canonized pope
59 Seer's gift
60 Ham's surroundings

22
leftovers
by dean niles

ACROSS

1 Barely sufficient
6 Branch of mythology
11 Paper handler
16 Shinto-temple gateway
17 Voltaire or Elia
18 Stallone's avenger
19 Came to mind
20 Suit
21 Remove, in a way
22 Top-rated film of '93
25 Part of AD
26 Cast off
27 S&L offering
29 Game, __ and match
31 School of whales
34 *Niño*'s aunt
36 Biblical priest
38 Zinc __ (ointment ingredient)
41 Orts
45 Blake's rank on *M*A*S*H*
46 Plain Jane of fiction
47 It's spotted in Texas
48 CDs' ancestors
50 Bowler, but not golfer
51 Small piece
52 __ *Mater* (hymn)
55 GI offense
57 Shoe material

61 Certain store's specialty
63 Locke form
64 Budget-chart shape
65 "To __ their golden eyes": Shak.
66 6-pt. plays
68 Friend of Fidel
69 VH-1 rival
71 Unoccupied
74 Hammett hound
77 Guess Who tune of '70
83 Phonograph needles

85 "Fighting vainly the old __": Cole Porter
86 Geena Davis film of '94
87 Wears
88 Spin __ (exaggerate)
89 Leaf pore
90 Special edition
91 Renais-sance poet
92 Monopoly prop

DOWN

1 Sky light
2 Nuclear-reactor part

3 Like benzene
4 Hebrew month
5 Advertising gimmick
6 Catches
7 Bread spread
8 Jazz phrases
9 Biblical verb
10 Discerning sort
11 Gunk
12 Polynesian porch
13 Of the sky
14 Barry Bonds stat.
15 __-*Tiki*

23 Yuletide drink
24 Friend of Ford
28 Ken-L Ration competitor
29 Impresario Hurok
30 Add'l phone
32 Put away
33 Perchance
35 Point a finger at
37 -arian relative
39 Sound-system name
40 City near Fort Bliss
42 Street fight

43 Alter, perhaps
44 *Concentration* puzzle
49 "Keep it simple, __"
52 Drain
53 Auto ornamenta-tion
54 February birthstone
56 Dr. Leary's "prescrip-tion"
58 French seafood
59 "Camptown Races" syllable
60 Pinkerton's logo
62 Beef, for instance
67 Japanese honorific
70 Courage
72 Weill's wife
73 Ferber and Millay
75 Swagger
76 Scout's rider
78 15th-century ship
79 Something we share
80 Port authority?
81 Lawn chemical
82 Do business
83 __-*Devil* (Streep film)
84 Put a strain on

23

silly songs

by dean niles

ACROSS

1 Shakespearean plotter
5 Plane spotter
10 Brando's brother in *On the Waterfront*
17 Reason out
18 Greek marketplace
19 Helena's home
20 Stevie Wonder tune of '68
23 Russian space station
24 Intense loathing
25 Geological periods
26 Chowed down
27 Wine word
29 __-Kamenogorsk (Kazakh city)
30 "__ My Hand In" (*Hello, Dolly!* tune)
32 Still sleeping
33 Hank Ballard tune of '61
38 "Goodness!"
40 Carol season
41 __-flytrap
44 Kafkaesque
47 Eating alcove
48 Tennyson hero
49 Nothing but
51 Unit of fluidity
52 Clinton's instrument
53 *Song of the South* tune
58 Peyton Place's main street
61 Bustle
62 Submit, with "out"
63 Bwana, in Bengal
67 Vile
70 Radioactivity, essentially

72 *Saturday Night Fever* director
73 "¿*Cómo* __ *usted?*"
76 '30s film legend
77 Manfred Mann tune of '64
81 Passed easily
83 Porcine plaint
84 Perking place
85 Dictionary abbr.
87 "And __ the opposite shore will be"
88 Indomitable spirit
90 Stradivari's teacher

92 Feeling off
94 Little Anthony & The Imperials tune of '60
99 Easygoing
100 Take back to court
101 French pronoun
102 Driving machines
103 What's really the matter?
104 Goes out with

DOWN

1 "God created man __ image"
2 Ahead of time, old-style
3 Prefix for thermal

4 Deprived: It.
5 Salad ingredient
6 Rabbitlike rodent
7 Dire destiny
8 Wall Street trader, for short
9 Actress __ Dawn Chong
10 Honey-tongued
11 Animated character
12 Pass catchers
13 Call __ day
14 Social butterflies
15 Related on Mom's side
16 Emanated, in a way
17 Distinctive doctrine

21 Draws forth
22 Low card
28 Town near Mesa Verde National Park
30 Letters of credit?
31 DC type
32 Top-rated
34 Muscat resident
35 Economic pattern
36 Like college walls
37 A hundred yrs.
38 Graduate deg.
39 Portion of corn
42 __-Puf (fabric softener)
43 Dr. Ruth's specialty
45 Apple-polisher
46 __-China

47 Gandhi garb
50 Thus far
51 Leeway
54 Majorca's capital
55 Apprehension
56 Syrian statesman
57 Beehive, for one
58 Flow away
59 Perrins' partner
60 Exasperating
64 Gideons' offering
65 Diminutive suffix
66 Social worker's deg.
68 Did a smithy's job
69 "I tawt I __ a puddy tat!"
71 Japanese belief
73 Head of Hollywood
74 Trespass
75 Audiotape maker
78 Raises the flag
79 "That was delicious!"
80 Ducklings' dads
81 Plane pathway
82 Hebrew priest
86 Plum relatives
88 Feds
89 Baseball star Sandberg
90 "Are not!" response
91 Eisenhower's namesakes
93 Some records
95 DI doubled
96 George's brother/collaborator
97 Shook hands with
98 Word a toreador adores

24
beau jest
by dean niles

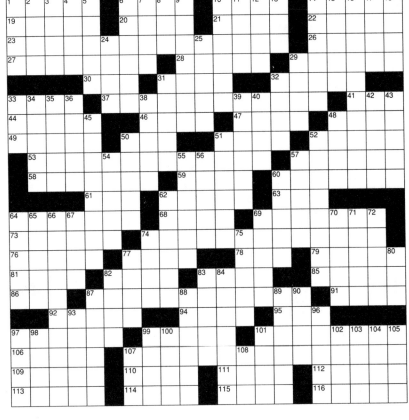

ACROSS

1 Great divide
6 Pro __
10 1/2 fl. oz.
14 Lively dance
19 Supplement
20 A part of
21 Groundbreaking tools
22 Have __ to pick
23 Beau's business?
26 Cranks the clock
27 Conscious
28 Zionism founder
29 Contraption
30 Turkish topper
31 King's address
32 Misfortune
33 Smug look
37 Munchkin's beau?
41 Typesetting widths
44 Stockdale's running-mate
46 Lumbering sort
47 Mideast King
48 *Inter* __
49 Take down a peg
50 Canine comment
51 Behold, to Brutus
52 Swindle
53 Beau's kiss?
57 Arthurian chronicler
58 __ manner (doctor's deportment)
59 Edda character
60 Post-WWII antagonism
61 Poetic preposition
62 Winter covering
63 Lime cooler
64 Pledges
68 Actor Julia
69 Come before
73 Spa setups
74 Beau's spy?
76 Dickinson of *Police Woman*
77 Indian butter
78 Increases
79 Free partner

81 Straight, at the bar
82 Clinton, in headlines
83 Cadabra preceder
85 Wound up
86 Incoming plane: Abbr.
87 How beaus like their steaks?
91 Tolstoy's turndown
92 Chicago mayor
94 Dramatic conflict
95 Pre-NRC grp.
97 Got away, old-style
99 North Dakota city
101 Relic from the past

106 Pianist Watts
107 Beau's farewell?
109 Frolicsome
110 __ Eleanor Roosevelt
111 A Four Corners state
112 Mural beginning
113 Panache
114 Gallivant
115 Cereal spokestiger
116 It may be ruled

DOWN

1 Comic actress Peggy
2 Nuts-and-bolts business: Abbr.
3 Gulf of __ (Arabian Sea arm)
4 Dele undoer

5 Recurring theme
6 Wagner opera
7 Medical-school subj.
8 Rocky peak
9 Colony's construction
10 Eric's sobriquet
11 Ruth's husband
12 Deal in
13 Ltr. addenda
14 King Arthur's nephew
15 Put up with
16 Beau's favorite poet?
17 "Somebody bet __ bay"
18 Pain in the neck
24 Achilles' sore spot

25 *The Ten Commandments* star
29 Electrical-distribution network
31 Things
32 Stamp backing
33 Some MDs
34 Occupational therapist's work
35 Bent out of shape
36 Itinerant
38 Violent struggle
39 Mongolfiers' achievement
40 Slightly improper
42 Millionths of a meter
43 Attendant of Bacchus
45 Mosaic tiles
48 "__ Lang Syne"

50 Mosquito genus
51 Set apart, in a way
52 Put a curse on
54 Spares, for example
55 Roman odist
56 Sussex scent
57 Computer accessory
60 Kings and queens
62 Cop's command
64 Yoga posture
65 More sensible
66 Beau's favorite candy?
67 Troop troupe
69 Kind of bull
70 "Stormy Weather" composer
71 Lilliputian
72 Strike out
74 Ark occupant
75 Italy's Detroit
77 Reb's color
80 Part of AARP
82 Beseeched
83 Special vocabulary
84 Evict
87 Jason's quest
88 Small chicken
89 Coarse, as humor
90 Art __
93 Shower time
96 Loft group
97 Maglie and Mineo
98 11th-century king
99 Not stereo
100 One of the Inner Hebrides
101 __ impasse
102 Element's ID
103 :, in math
104 Salutation
105 Substantial content
107 Coal product
108 Oklahoma Indian

randolph ross

High-school principal. Home: New York

Previous Occupation
High-school math teacher.

Education
B.A. in mathematics (minor in English and education) from Queens College (New York, NY), M.A. in mathematics from Columbia University, M.A. in educational administration from Columbia University.

Crossword Credentials
First crossword accepted for publication in *Newsday* in 1988. Creator of the crossword for *First for Women* magazine since 1989. Regular contributor to *The New York Times*, the *Newsday* crossword, the Uptown Puzzle Club, and numerous puzzle magazines.

Many puzzlers think that they should be able to construct crosswords simply because they've solved so many of them. By that line of reasoning, years of listening to classical music should provide all the training necessary to compose a symphony. In reality, puzzlemakers undergo a period of "apprenticeship" before their skills are developed enough to create publishable work. This usually involves working with a friendly editor, learning the many rules that are not at all obvious from solving crosswords. With only one exception, every crossword I've ever received from a beginner has had at least one flaw that prevented its being considered for publication.

Randy Ross's first puzzle was that one exception. Not only was it technically flawless, it had an eye-popping theme. Appearing in the Sunday edition of *Newsday* six years ago, its title was "One Good Turn." Among the theme answers were ROULETTE WHEELS, TURNS AROUND and SEMICIRCLE. But what made the puzzle remarkable was the phrase that appeared in the center of the puzzle. In the shape of a square, to be read clockwise from the upper left, was ROUND AND ROUND SHE GOES, WHERE SHE STOPS, NOBODY KNOWS.

As a young solver in the '60s, Randy admired the puzzles of the late Jack Luzzatto, who was well known for his wide-open patterns. Randy is also known for wide-open puzzles, but his four *Masterpiece* crosswords show the great diversity of his skills.

Puzzle #25 - "Unthemed"
It's rare for a puzzle this size to have more than six answers of nine letters or more – this one has 14! A diverse gathering of celebrities, phrases, and interesting facts.

Puzzle #26 - "Ambiguous Occupations"
The five theme answers include two pairs in consecutive rows.

Puzzle #27 - "Quoteword Puzzle"
There are other puzzles with quotations in this book, but none like this. This is a crossword variety invented by Randy, with one *word* going in each box of 8 Down. You'll have to write some of the words smaller than usual to fit them in.

Puzzle #28 - "Queueing In"
A puzzle remarkable for the letter of the alphabet highlighted, as well as the tight consistency of the theme. Note how each "punny" answer has the same relationship to the "straight" version of the answer.

25
unthemed
by randolph ross

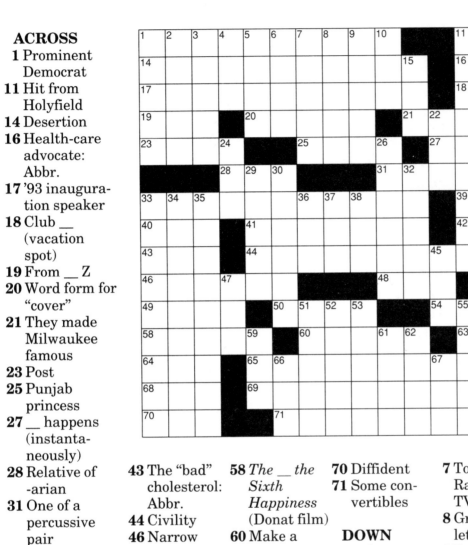

ACROSS
1 Prominent Democrat
11 Hit from Holyfield
14 Desertion
16 Health-care advocate: Abbr.
17 '93 inauguration speaker
18 Club __ (vacation spot)
19 From __ Z
20 Word form for "cover"
21 They made Milwaukee famous
23 Post
25 Punjab princess
27 __ happens (instantaneously)
28 Relative of -arian
31 One of a percussive pair
33 Drives discourteously
39 Civil War veterans org.
40 "__ to Extremes" (Billy Joel tune)
41 Bring about
42 Otolaryngologist's specialty: Abbr.

43 The "bad" cholesterol: Abbr.
44 Civility
46 Narrow shelves
48 Understand
49 Snick-and-__ knife
50 __ Baltimore ('70s sitcom)
54 "Take __ song and make it better"

58 *The __ the Sixth Happiness* (Donat film)
60 Make a second request
63 Make a blunder
64 Small amount
65 Do December decorating
68 Spanish pronoun
69 *Carrie* author

70 Diffident
71 Some convertibles

DOWN
1 __ boy (sissy)
2 Let up
3 Polyester partner
4 __ Ray Hutton (Big Band name)
5 Harem rooms
6 Afr. or Eur.

7 Tony Randall TV role
8 Greek letter
9 Breakfast fruit
10 "Sail __ Ship of State!"
11 *The African Queen* screenwriter
12 Yanks
13 Undesirable first impressions

15 Margarine holder
22 Musical discernment
24 Insult, in today's slang
26 What you see
29 Western transport
30 Do a grain processing job
32 Designer Simpson
33 Slopes
34 Light versifier
35 Odets play
36 East ender
37 Snitch
38 Small bill
45 Tchrs.' lobby
47 GM car
51 Bay window
52 Arizona State city
53 Wood-shop machine
55 Letter flourish
56 Amphitheater center
57 Bottom of the barrel
59 One-point NBA plays
61 Name for a police dog
62 Kesey and Berry
66 ACLU concern
67 Boxing result

26
ambiguous occupations
by randolph ross

ACROSS
1 Giraffe kin
6 General Arnold's nickname
9 Something boring
13 Home helper or marine sentinel
18 Putting experts or short driving experts
19 Roasting places
20 Pooh pal
21 River deposit
22 Joins forces
24 Boo-boo
25 Noise made by a fan?
27 Statistics
29 Xmas time
32 Joins the audience
37 Sandinista leader
39 Lady Chaplin
40 Atka native
42 *Them* author
43 Miniature or chattering emcee
47 Proscription
48 League members
49 Escape routes
50 Donahue of *Father Knows Best*
52 Bib needers
54 Slow down, in mus.

55 Canasta combination
58 Patty Hearst's kidnappers: Abbr.
59 Signal via pager
61 Tycoon's digs
66 Loving sounds
70 Decadent
73 Manufactured soap
74 Well-built or Honda salesmen
77 Diminutive or O. Henry reciter

78 Protein-rich bean
79 Switch settings
80 "Now I __ down . . ."

DOWN
1 Green shade
2 Pirate Hall-of-Famer
3 How wines become great
4 *Star Trek* weaponry
5 *Addams Family* cousin
6 Long and Lewis

7 "Nothing makes you feel as good __" (ad slogan)
8 City on the Illinois river
9 Super, in today's slang
10 Agents, for short
11 Start of the second qtr.
12 Earth sci.
14 Shade
15 You can dig it
16 Pilferer, for short
17 Queue after Q

18 Familiar taxi-service operator
23 Peace Nobelist of '78
26 Greetings from Granada
28 ". . . and pretty maids all in __"
29 Unwelcome road sign
30 Spews out
31 Acting companies
32 Mogadishu man
33 Shortly
34 Toucan's toenail

35 Shoemaker's strip
36 Used the microwave
38 South Lake __, CA
39 Kitchen-appliance name
41 Absolute ruler
44 Await ominously
45 Some Blue Cross cos.
46 "__ Mio"
51 Violin's ancestors
53 Where *Madama Butterfly* premiered
56 "There's nothing __ say"
57 Military alert status
60 Nectar sources
62 Reckoning
63 Basketball star Olajuwon
64 Ground, in Grenoble
65 *N.Y. Times* execs.
66 Hypo units
67 __ and aahs
68 Melville romance
69 Like gymnasts
71 Take a crack at
72 Cleve. clock setting
75 __ standstill
76 Slippery swimmer

27

quoteword puzzle

by randolph ross

ACROSS

1 Prone to imitation
6 *Sweet Bird __* (Williams play)
9 Talk and talk and talk and talk and talk and . . .
12 Stroller pushers, often
16 Creator of Jane and Hercule
17 Changes the decor
18 Part of some GIs' addresses
19 Graven image
20 Choir platforms
21 Footnote writer
23 Dover dish
24 __ minimum (no less than)
25 School founded in 1440
27 Well-informed
29 Misbehaving
30 Cub-scout group
31 What "i.e." means
32 Take by force
33 Road, in old Rome
35 Popular topper of the '20s
38 Hold back
40 Marine-seismologist's device
42 Montgomery and his peers
43 Bass product
44 Exchange
48 Exchange
49 Very nearly
50 Sally in space
52 Sen. Heflin's state
53 Ancient Peruvian
56 Mental giant
58 __ room (family place)

59 Aetna competitor
64 How long a play plays
65 Movie genre
66 IRS agent, e.g.
67 Roam aimlessly
68 Disencumbers
69 Hypothetical question
71 Stiff winds
75 Telltale sign
77 Take-home
78 "__ Grand Old Flag"
80 *South Pacific* hero
81 Beginning
83 How the 27 Across speak
85 French summers
86 *A Bell for __*

89 Selective Service System, in the '60s
91 __ Lingus
93 Stowe girl
94 Capturer's comment
97 "Alice's Restaurant" name
98 L.A. NFLer
99 Gulf sultanate
100 Seer, for one
102 Spot
104 The Pharisees, e.g.
105 Vein contents
106 Something to gossip about
107 Relatives on Mom's side
108 Oil giant of yore

109 __ & *Stimpy* (cartoon show)
110 Cat's hangout
111 Take a second?

DOWN

1 Washing-machine part
2 Rose Bowl's home
3 Mineralogist's suffix
4 Scintilla
5 Rash actions
6 Locale of Camus' *The Plague*
7 Marshy area
8 19-word quote from *The New Speaker's Handbook*
9 Microsoft magnate

10 Like two peas in __
11 Five-time Wimbledon winner
12 Takes by surprise
13 Southwest building material
14 *Valley of the __* (Susann bestseller)
15 Winter forecast
16 Middle East expert
22 Ryan's *Love Story* costar
26 Being broadcast
28 Lea lady
34 Spokes
36 Long, narrow inlet

37 Snoozing
38 Most cunning
39 Monotony
41 Apartment dweller
43 Part of MA
45 Tip off
46 One of the Baldwin brothers
47 Tempo
51 Stir to anger
54 Slot spot
55 Start of a children's song
57 Swift specialty
59 Logician's conjunction
60 Campus area
61 Bring to naught
62 Shoemaker's shape
63 "What's in __?"
70 Did the catering
72 Well-read
73 High
74 Tropical plants
76 Met
79 Winglike
82 British gold coin, for short
84 Old __ (Disney dog)
86 Narrow winning margin
87 Architectural hemispheres
88 US spy plane
89 Poet Mark Van __
90 Hwy.
92 Network exec Arledge
95 Get an __ effort
96 *Earth in the Balance* author
97 The Cadets
101 Shoe-box letters
103 Cornfield comment

28

queueing in
by randolph ross

ACROSS

1 Portable bed
4 Made cubes out of
9 Master strokes
14 Mme. of Malaga
17 Busy mo. for the IRS
18 Better ventilated
19 Refuges
20 Area meas.
21 Evidence in the mollusk case?
23 Exerciser's exclamation?
25 Gritty
26 Memorable Gary Cooper role
27 Prefix for official
28 Capote's nickname
29 Most widely grown nut
32 __ gum (ice-cream ingredient)
33 John Marshall's milk?
37 New Year's Day events
40 Sweet snacks
41 Puniest pups
42 *The Merry __* (Lehar work)
43 That: Fr.
45 Antoine Domino's nickname
46 Inkling
47 Magazine exhortation
48 Study all night
49 Stout relative
50 Super sovereign?
52 Elizabethan playhouse
53 Forthright
54 Strike callers
55 Mason's tool
56 Most lanky
59 Like dishwater
61 Military shelter
62 Loath
63 Full of energy
64 Geometric drawing
65 Spells
66 Wobbly dessert?
69 Half a figure-eight
72 College course of study
73 *Wheel of Fortune* turns
74 A day in Dijon
75 America's westernmost point
76 Oath response
77 Not appropriate
78 He goes to court
79 Peer
80 *A Touch __* ('73 film)
82 Mr. Spock's peculiar superior?
84 One-liner
85 Clairol rival
86 René's "Okay"
87 Foreign-car make
89 Nautical direction
91 Speechless
95 Resigning scout?
97 Part of Bartlett's outfit?
100 Samovars
101 Cool it
102 All-inclusive
103 Galoot
104 King __ Saud
105 Starch source, informally
106 Word on a $1 bill
107 To date

DOWN

1 Hernando's house
2 Alphabetic sequence
3 Fine-tune
4 Chinese hors d'oeuvres
5 *"Dies __"*
6 Geom. figure
7 "A mouse!"
8 Denton et al.
9 Convincingly stated
10 Propelled, perhaps
11 Secondhand
12 Mendel's specialty
13 Concorde
14 Uncool cornfield sentinels?
15 Inlets
16 Protesting
18 Really goes for
20 Smallest military unit
22 Lead-ins
24 __ Valley, ID
26 '50s actress Diana
29 Old MacDonald heard it
30 Something businesspeople "do"
31 Brit's buddy
32 Wax
33 Parlor piece
34 Russian river
35 Singer Seeger
36 Like some knights
37 Reforestation specimens
38 Capital of Yemen
39 Navy builder
42 Prone to cry
44 Atlantic fish
46 Poke fun at
47 Beef cut
48 He may be beside himself
50 An estate
51 Berth places
52 Orange's origin
53 Sets off
55 Asian language group
56 Irani religion
57 Carry too far
58 *Zorba the Greek* star's relatives?
59 Exhausted
60 Vein contents
61 Lateral leader
63 Sends off
64 Wedge-shaped
66 Books experts
67 Emulate Romeo and Juliet
68 Salesman's goal
69 Word in the etymology of "tweezers"
70 Headliner
71 Pout
73 Cereal sound
75 Altair's constellation
77 Of the hipbone
78 Toad feature
79 Liken
81 Sportscaster Gowdy et al.
82 Where Hollywood meets Vine
83 Observant ones
85 Untethered
87 *"__ se habla español"*
88 Restrain
89 Neck of the woods
90 H.S. jrs.' exam
91 Take a crack __
92 Slick
93 Pivot
94 One of the NCOs
96 False front
97 Proof-ending initials
98 Arles article
99 Racetrack alternative: Abbr.

karen hodge

High-school French teacher. Home: Connecticut

Previous Occupation
Social director for a military service club.

Education
B.A. in French from Connecticut College (New London), M.A. in Liberal Studies from Wesleyan University (Middletown, CT).

Crossword Credentials
First crossword published in *The Four-Star Puzzler* (puzzle newsletter formerly published by *Games* magazine) in 1983. Has directed an annual crossword-solving contest since 1988 for the benefit of a local library. Has been widely published in puzzle magazines.

Since Karen has been relatively inactive as a puzzlemaker in the last few years, you may not be familiar with her crosswords. But she is one of America's most talented constructors, and I was fortunate to persuade her to come out of semi-retirement to participate in this book. Karen is best-known for her humorous themes; all four of her *Masterpiece* puzzles fall into that category, with the theme clues in all her puzzles followed by question marks. She is looking forward to making more puzzles, including cryptic crosswords, in the near future.

Puzzle #29 - "Pay Up!"
You owe it to yourself to chuckle over the subject matter.

Puzzle #30 - "My Mind Is Racing"
There are six theme answers in this puzzle, including two pairs that intersect each other. A few Executive Branch references will be found among the nontheme answers, but one clue that looks like it should be one, isn't.

Puzzle #31 - "Pardon My French"
Given her profession, Karen has probably been collecting puns like these for a long time.

Puzzle #32 - "Themes Like Old Times"
A clever title for a puzzle whose ten theme answers should be pronounced in order to be appreciated.

29
pay up!
by karen hodge

ACROSS
1 Close with force
5 Young snorter
9 Chocolate center
14 Hemingway sobriquet
15 Assert
16 Attacked
17 Buddy who's buying in Brisbane?
19 Adult insect
20 Mysterious
21 Nicotinic acid, for one
23 Scandinavian toast
24 Battery metal
25 Walt Kelly's creation
27 Fell apart under pressure
32 Emirate resident
36 Gimlet or screwdriver
38 Make __ (succeed financially)
39 Melodramatic
41 Just like
42 *The War Between the __* (Lurie bestseller)
43 François' farewell
44 Olive-branch bearer

46 Soup vegetable
47 Word-processor function
49 Stare open-mouthed
51 Girl in a 1918 tune
53 Ottomans' religion
57 Proficient
61 Tanshui River city
63 Suspect's story
64 Statement seeker?

67 Triple-A recommen-dation
68 Grimm villain
69 Alterna-tively
70 Play for time
71 Cool
72 Deli loaves

DOWN
1 Humane org.
2 Comic Bert's family

3 "A Bushel and __" (*Guys and Dolls* tune)
4 Portuguese territory
5 Broadway smash of '60
6 Eggs
7 Stand for
8 Famous fountain
9 Conversa-tion about debt?
10 Hindu avatar

11 Nether-lands export
12 Biblical trio
13 007 alma mater
18 Prefix for sack
22 Small-business magazine
24 Frequent *Jeopardy!* category
26 Stir up
28 Gemstone found in New Mexico

29 Hawk relative
30 "Waiting for the Robert __"
31 Office furniture
32 "Sorry to hear that!"
33 Not at all civil
34 Oratorio solo
35 *Oktoberfest* quaff
37 Hot stuff
40 What deadbeats do?
45 Nickname
48 *Henry IV* prince
50 Birthright barterer
52 Grand __ National Park
54 Phonograph sleeve
55 Properly
56 Part of Reagan's inner circle
57 Mechanical cylinders
58 Greatly
59 Falafel adjunct
60 Steel-union boss I.W.
62 Makes mad
65 Epoch
66 Swimsuit part

30
my mind is racing
by karen hodge

ACROSS

1 Sherman's hell
4 Preacher at Nineveh
9 Unwanted stuff
14 Operate in the red
15 Met standards
17 No longer edible
19 Syncopated style
20 Early recording star
21 Genoan statesman Doria
22 Night-racing equipment?
25 Sleeve contents
26 Consequently
27 Draft-card org.
28 Knock it off
29 Detailed procedures: Abbr.
33 Issue at hand
35 __ Alamos, NM
38 Rodeo Drive attractions
40 Naomi, to Wynonna
43 College major
44 __ for Humanity (home-building charity)
47 Saccharine
48 Polo of Venice
50 Do away with
51 Police phone job
52 Shed __ for (bemoan)
53 Last word of *"Adeste Fideles"*
55 Adams, Johnson or Carter
56 Begins a fight
58 Pop singer LaBelle
59 Eye sore
60 Zodiacal spots
62 Big slipknot
64 Hardness-scale name
66 Poetic adverb
68 Coolidgelike
72 Subj. for recent immigrants
73 Ideal racing participants?
78 Sour-tasting
80 Collegian's quest
81 __-relief
82 Consort of Titus Andronicus
83 Indulgent periods
84 Simile center
85 Wheel on a spur
86 Bursts (with)
87 Love-neigh-bor link

DOWN

1 Valued at
2 Informed
3 '80s Treasury Secretary
4 Racing two-reelers?
5 Pearly stone
6 Saint Philip __
7 Cut __ (dance)
8 Breakfast side dish
9 Door topper
10 Called up
11 Plus
12 Where racing cancella-tions are noted?
13 Word form for "sacred"
16 Barflies
18 A bit wet
23 Hypo units
24 Relative of -arian
28 Shankar's specialty
30 __ Na Na
31 "And so __": Pepys
32 Hubert's successor
34 Race-starting lady?
35 Shangri-La officials
36 Do a declamation
37 How ritzy jockeys get to the finish line?
39 PAID or PLEASE REMIT
41 Orlando attraction
42 Town near Greenwich, CT
45 Thai or Turk
46 Nearing the hour
49 __ belli
54 __-Aztecan (Indian language family)
57 Special effect, in film slang
61 Haggard novel
63 A foot wide?
64 Gist
65 Dorian's creator
67 Early automaker
69 Muhammad V University locale
70 Huge success
71 Emerson opus
73 Shoot off
74 Part of LAPD
75 Folklore meanie
76 On the house
77 Regard
79 Jones' partner

31
pardon my french
by karen hodge

ACROSS
1 Perfume base
6 Caviar source
10 Material mishap
13 Tacks on
17 Transparent linen
18 __ Alto, CA
19 72 Across, for instance
20 Schnitzel, essentially
21 Corruption in municipal government?
23 Tying tale?
25 Swimmer in the news in '26
26 Ballroom steps
28 Readied the presses
29 Half a literary pseudonym
31 Imported auto
32 Horton hatched one
33 Ayatollah's realm
36 Pair
38 Bell man
40 *The New Diplomacy* author
44 Young fellow
45 Last of the Mohicans' neighbors?
48 Big name in PC's
49 Jacket fabric
51 __ Pan Alley
52 Wayside stop
53 Don't play it straight
54 Standish stand-in
55 October birthstone
58 Intricate assemblage
60 Mideast ruler
62 Rubensian subjects
64 Corduroy rib
65 Engraved
68 Carryall
69 Assail
72 "__ Skylark"
73 Madame Butterfly's sash
74 Egypt/Syr. alliance of yore
76 Fictional Thompson
77 Cash-filled convenience: Abbr.
78 Suffering from writer's cramp?
83 Dad's bro
84 Nomadic Finn
86 Pen resident
87 Pilot's hdg.
88 Clockmaker Thomas
89 Churchill's "so few"
91 Exxon rival
93 Swing support, sometimes
95 Shower time
98 Treat meat
100 Chatter noisily
104 Diplomatic sweet talk?
107 Tough time at the office?
109 Cartographic speck
110 Must pay
111 Sport blade
112 Put up
113 Makes a hue turn?
114 Performed nuptials
115 Pygmalion's sister
116 Comic actress Taylor

DOWN
1 "Ma! He's Making Eyes __"
2 Despicable sort
3 Mah-jongg piece
4 Second man on the moon
5 Hoedown dances
6 Fitness center
7 Revolutionary War financier Solomon
8 "Half __ is better . . ."
9 African rodents
10 Of interest to Capek
11 Altar affirmation
12 Sanctuary seat
13 Settle a score
14 Editor's station
15 Frontpage feature?
16 Gravity powered vehicle
22 Victor at Gettysburg
24 Band engagement
27 Roseanne Arnold, née __
30 Waldheim or Weill
32 By this time
33 *Casablanca* heroine
34 Actor Julia
35 Soldiers' refresher?
37 Pizza topping
39 Rock star Clapton
41 Expected lodging?
42 Rose Mary Murphy's love
43 Fifth-largest st.
45 Eisenhower's birthplace
46 Database fodder
47 As one
50 Mrs. Bruce Willis
56 Hoo-ha
57 Abate
59 Bargain, perhaps
61 Snub
63 Tapes shut
65 Attention-getting type: Abbr.
66 __ care in the world
67 Where Mercury could be seen in the '30s
70 Isn't wrong?
71 Word in engineering school names
75 "If I rest, I __"
79 "%#@&#%!!"
80 Student quarters
81 Turned PEOPLE into XJZXKJ
82 Gallic gratitude
85 Lion groups
88 Out of danger
90 "Pale" potable
92 Long-tongued mammal
94 Rarin' to go
95 Battery liquid
96 Bouquet
97 Characterization
99 Looked over
101 Razor-sharp
102 *The Women* writer
103 *Harper's Bazaar* cover artist
105 Drag along
106 Wide-eyed reaction
108 Auto of the '20s

32
themes like old times
by karen hodge

ACROSS

1 Alternating-current innovator
6 Unchatty sort
10 CD-player device
15 Cut down to size
19 John of rock
20 Horne or Olin
21 Seneca's stars
22 Superboy's girlfriend
23 Sermon topic?
25 Digital count?
27 Tourist's reference
28 *Ben-__*
29 National League division
31 Like __ out of hell
32 Frost preposition
33 Many MTV watchers
36 Beatty/Hoffman film of '87
40 Play the ponies
43 New World legend?
47 Land in *Normandie*
48 Holy Roman Emperor
50 On __ with (equivalent to)
51 *The Once and Future King* author's monogram
52 Authoritative decree
53 Poker pile
55 Night-school subj.
56 Tigger's friend
57 Key letter
58 Italian noble
59 Sandal manual?
63 Not as ruddy
65 Some Greenlanders
67 Lunar expanse
68 From Sidon
70 Frosting user
71 One side of a turn-of-the-century war

73 Spill the beans
74 Last-round player
78 First name in spydom
79 Altar attendant
82 Emulate Izaak Walton
83 *Ghostbusters* sedan?
86 Gas-powered cycle
87 *Mission: Impossible* org.
88 Helping hand
89 Crude quarters
90 Betraying awe
91 Way to go
94 Virus component
95 Help on a heist
97 British carbine

98 "Rule Britannia" composer's family
99 Big talker?
104 Bucks and stags
105 Cool and collected
107 Defunct alliance
108 Call a bluff, maybe
109 Delta material
111 Frying medium
113 Tarzan of TV
114 Schedule C expert
117 Where to buy algebra books?
122 Anorectic?
125 Tub in the fridge
126 Bedevil
127 Shade close to bone
128 "Venice of the Orient"
129 Road Runner's remark

130 Aspirin is one
131 Cloverleaf segment
132 Surprise win

DOWN

1 Coworkers
2 Island off Italy
3 What to do when you see red
4 Bud's buddy
5 Olympic-medal music
6 Product of Bordeaux
7 Ring around the collar
8 Pot starter
9 Sanskrit for "high-souled one"
10 Second of two
11 Last of the log
12 VW forerunners
13 Columnist Bombeck

14 Harry Kemelman's sleuth
15 Not naked
16 Traitor
17 "__ clear day . . ."
18 Crony
24 Last word in a Faulkner title
26 Sample
30 He gets what's coming
34 Safecracker's "soup"
35 Flounder flock
37 Side-road choice?
38 McDonald's trademark
39 Call it a day
40 Lawn game
41 Group spirit
42 Scholarship money?
44 Jumbled mess
45 Self-possession
46 Came to

49 Word in eyeglass-store names
54 Bacchus' mother
55 French connections
60 Ruth's in-law
61 Vast
62 Wharf space
63 Pablo's daughter
64 Similar things
66 "It must be him, __ shall die"
69 English channel?
72 Algonquian chief
74 "__ a star, when only one . . .": Wordsworth
75 "__ ways than one!"
76 Honey bunch
77 Singer Lopez et al.
79 Oils, for instance
80 Cheyenne shelter
81 Barbara and Anthony
84 Old saying
85 Wheels
92 Canterbury café
93 Approx. cost
95 "__ girl!"
96 __ of the court (legal-notice phrase)
100 Type of top
101 Exhausted
102 Follow up a kiss?
103 "Psst!"
106 Make happy
110 Chic modifier
112 Metric prefix
114 Part of Addams' signature
115 He reached his peak
116 Biol. branch
117 Riotous crowd
118 Stout alternative
119 Placekicker's prop
120 *Krazy __*
121 Gazetteer abbr.
123 Activate, as a fuze
124 1/8 fl. oz.

emily cox & henry rathvon

Professional crossword creators. Home: Pennsylvania

Previous Occupations
Emily: Troubleshooter for an acoustical engineering company (the company that analyzed the JFK assassination and Watergate tapes). Henry: House painter, dishwasher, doorman.

Education
Emily: Attended Tufts University. Henry: B.A. in English from Bennington College, M.A. in education from Tufts University.

Crossword Credentials
Editors of *The Four-Star Puzzler* (early '80s). Creators of the *Atlantic Monthly* Puzzler since 1977. Co-creators of the *Boston Globe* Sunday crossword since 1978. Contributing editors to numerous puzzle magazines.

Best known nationally for their *Atlantic* cryptic crosswords, Emily and Henry don't consider themselves particularly "masterful" creators of American-style crosswords. When you've completed their puzzles, it's a safe bet that you'll disagree.

Puzzle #33 - "Give Up?"
The two theme answers at 9 and 32 Down provide hints to the phrase that will be found along the diagonal. The elegant final answer is a Cox/Rathvon trademark, especially in their *Atlantic Monthly* puzzles.

Puzzle #34 - "Playing with Words"
An introduction to "cryptic" crosswords. Each clue is in two parts: one, a definition of the answer (which may be a synonym or pun); the other, a form of wordplay designed to spell out the answer for you. The wordplay in this puzzle will be of one of these types:

ANAGRAM The letters of the answer are scrambled into one or more words within the clue. The use of anagrams is signaled by a word that suggests rearrangement or disorder.
CHARADE The answer is broken into two or more parts, each of which is given or clued.
DELETION The answer is derived by removing a letter from a longer word.
DOUBLE DEFINITION Two distinct meanings of the answer are defined.
HIDDEN The answer appears camouflaged within a word or phrase in the clue. This clue is signaled by a word that suggests concealment.
HOMOPHONE The answer sounds like a word or phrase given or clued, signaled by a word that suggests talking or speech.

Be sure to look over the explanations of each clue given in the back, whether or not you're able to solve them on your own. Once you understand how each of the clues in this puzzle works, you're on your way to becoming a cryptic puzzle fan!

Puzzle #35 - "At the Anagram Convention"
The title gives a hint to the nature of the nine theme answers. For fun, you might want to try coming up with other theme phrases of your own.

Puzzle #36 - "Hexagony"
A dazzler – hexagonal diagram, hexagonal "squares," and words going in *three* different directions. Despite the title (Hex-agony?), you shouldn't find this puzzle especially difficult. The clues are quite straightforward, and like regular crosswords, every letter is part of two different answers.

33

give up?

by emily cox & henry rathvon

ACROSS

1 Greek dawn goddess
4 Flirter with flame
8 Concorde fleet
12 Echidna hors d'oeuvres
14 Dresden's river
15 Double-cross
16 Go collectively ballistic
17 He loved Lucy
18 Pre-Nintendo giant
19 Disney's Herbie
21 Recorded blot
23 Approaches
24 "Stranger in Paradise" musical
25 Catcall?
27 Mortise connectors
30 Lhasa apso's origin
33 Earthy shade
35 Sworn statement
36 Say it's so
37 Slight reaction?
38 Old VCR format
39 Shoelace tip

40 Von Sydow's role in *The Greatest Story Ever Told*
41 Showy collection
42 Twenty Questions category
44 Make amends
46 Tops in beneficence
48 Don't blink
51 Security for Linus

53 End-zone activity
55 Basketball star Danny
56 Côte d'__ (French Riviera)
58 Home of the Bruins
59 Process ore
60 Creepy plant?
61 One fruit with the sound of two?
62 "Battle Hymn of the

Republic" author
63 A breeze
64 Tease

DOWN

1 Jazzman __ "Fatha" Hines
2 Pizza topping
3 Range in the home
4 Jellyfish
5 Designer Cassini
6 Atlanta super-station

7 Swiss miss
8 Glossy cloth
9 Go along with this puzzle's diagonal
10 Doughnuts, topologi-cally
11 Huff
13 Soft-shell clam
15 Door buster?
20 Liverpud-lian, e.g.
22 Lauder of fashion

24 Sour fruit
26 Gallic go-aheads
28 "__ creature was stirring . . ."
29 Bow with the wind
30 "Sayonara!"
31 A Karamazov
32 Go along with this puzzle's diagonal
34 Narc's operation
37 Martinique volcano
38 Laugh un-controllably
40 Record-album holder
41 Dead-set against
43 Be a good party-goer
45 Fish-hunting bird
47 Cooper's strip of wood
49 Masher alternative
50 Chou of China
51 Big party
52 Big wheel's big wheels
53 Phoenix hoopsters
54 Threads
57 Pakistani president

34

playing with words

by emily cox & henry rathvon

ACROSS

1 Our 14th President: Gore (6 letters)

4 Part of a dial that's not new (6,4)

10 Snakes – in summers (6)

11 Aladdin, in grooming, conceals eating place (6,4)

13 American Revolutionary, or a Lilliputian (6,3)

14 One of the R's, or one of Monopoly's railroads (7)

15 Lee & Chas. mixed up the Clintons' daughter (7)

16 Outlaw censored it? That's the way it sounds (6)

19 Something hot found in this tea mixture (5)

21 Rows or ranks, for crying out loud (5)

23 Thrower of a party suitable for kids – with a Whoopi Goldberg movie (5)

24 Anagram "Across" to get prizes (6)

26 Rearrange "letters" to spell "bridge" (7)

30 Held a watery scepter over the land? (7)

31 Overworked headline about Lugosi's ennui (9)

32 Puppet-show figure pronounced Warren

Beatty's intention re Ms. Bening (10)

33 Rockettes routine with two metal cylinders (6)

34 Circus boss who moonlights as a jewelry expert (10)

35 Seneca arranged for a medium setting (6)

DOWN

1 Druggist who's said to give ranch aid (10)

2 At risk: finish *Mad* (10)

3 Clergymen sure act out of order (7)

5 Sparkling water – it's natural when turned upside-down (5)

6 Greek character, possibly moronic when shaken up (7)

7 Erasing people's report cards? That's humiliating (9)

8 A handsome guy – like a British teacher is (6)

9 Injury that could make mother get gray hairs (6)

12 Tell what little rascals paint (6)

16 Grace is missing the second letter of the alphabet (5)

17 Decipher an acrostic for a Central American (5,5)

18 At 10:00, do a jig – all those present (10)

20 You'll do this if you claim "m" is not in "form" (9)

22 Sink to the bottom in Seattle, after dropping a letter (6)

25 Family of singing sisters aimlessly wanders (7)

27 Disorderly Reb came for a hug (7)

28 Earthquake upset Mr. Rote (6)

29 GI cereal for a Lebanese poet (6)

31 Flat-topped hill – a humdinger, by the sound of it (5)

35
at the anagram convention
by emily cox & henry rathvon

ACROSS

1 Rodin sculpture
8 Esau's alias
12 Aglaia, Euphrosyne, and Thalia
18 Fish like skipjacks
19 It shouldn't be done
20 Rhyme for "nevermore"
21 What Wyeth did at the convention?
23 Put in a box
24 Soul of a Parisian
25 What Day-Lewis did at the convention?
27 AAA handout
30 *The Great McGinty* director
32 Monty Python member
33 Tavern choices
35 One of the woodwinds
36 The stuff of double helixes
37 Dudley Do-Right's love
41 How Father's Day cards are addressed
43 Vaulted part of a church
45 Enlarge a hole
47 Andrea __ Sarto
48 Every third day
50 DeCarlo of *The Munsters*
52 Go a-courting
53 Shaggy ape
54 Noggin
55 Like old black and white movies
57 With 60 Across, what Ferraro did at the convention?

60 See 57 Across
62 Hasty hitcher
63 Effortlessly handled
65 "Don __ our gay . . ."
66 Iceberg extremity
67 One of the Borgias
69 Worshipful
72 Residential suffix
73 Despot
74 Draws a bead
77 Less screwy
78 Knight and Nugent
80 Promgoers: Abbr.
81 Half a spy's name
83 Word repeated in a Doris Day tune

84 Japanese indigene
86 Diana Ross was one
89 Perignon's title
90 What Marcos did at the convention?
94 "__ Lazy River"
96 Olive Oyl's brother
97 What Hopper did at the convention?
102 Jewish ascetic of old
103 Archaic "Holy cow!"
104 Metric land measure
105 Put away
106 Federal crimebuster
107 New Hampshire river

DOWN

1 Scheduler's "We'll let you know"
2 Darlin'
3 Receiver of bombs
4 *Star Trek: Deep Space Nine* character
5 What agendas comprise
6 Township near Johannesburg
7 Compass pt.
8 Inflames
9 Metaphysical poet
10 "__ the loneliest number"
11 Summary statistic

12 What actress Jackson did at the convention?
13 Kidney-related
14 Old, in Orléans
15 Iron-horse fodder
16 Scots Gaelic
17 Make rain by plane
22 __ in the bucket
26 Napkin material
27 Olympic swimmer Biondi
28 Healing plant
29 What explorer Cabral did at the convention?
31 River of Zaire
34 Old Persian governor
36 Unbusy bee
38 What Meese did at the convention?

39 Sierra __
40 *Safety Last* star
42 Regional lingo
44 Pupil's place
46 Spanish sheep
49 What Segovia did at the convention?
51 What "prices may" do
54 Tolerate
56 Classical markets
57 Grasp the point
58 The ritzy bunch
59 Draws close
61 "What __ of time!"
64 Vast expanse
68 New __ (Salisbury, England)
70 One of Seneca's students
71 About 1/28 ounce
75 Looms on the horizon
76 *Lundi* follower
79 NaCl seller
82 Entertains
85 "What on Earth have __?"
86 Prolonged battle
87 Arm bones
88 Long, long stories
90 Frosty treats
91 Pole on board
92 Old gas station sign
93 Capital of Yemen
95 Opposition member
98 Cable network, in TV listings
99 Forty winks
100 Before, lyrically
101 It may be doubled after "fiddle"

36
hexagony
by emily cox & henry rathvon

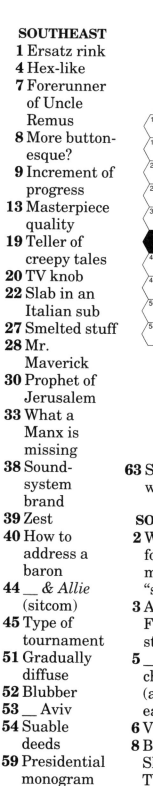

SOUTHEAST
1 Ersatz rink
4 Hex-like
7 Forerunner of Uncle Remus
8 More button-esque?
9 Increment of progress
13 Masterpiece quality
19 Teller of creepy tales
20 TV knob
22 Slab in an Italian sub
27 Smelted stuff
28 Mr. Maverick
30 Prophet of Jerusalem
33 What a Manx is missing
38 Sound-system brand
39 Zest
40 How to address a baron
44 __ & *Allie* (sitcom)
45 Type of tournament
51 Gradually diffuse
52 Blubber
53 __ Aviv
54 Suable deeds
59 Presidential monogram

63 Some sand-wiches

SOUTH
2 Word form meaning "sight"
3 Air France stopover
5 __ the chance (accept eagerly)
6 Vitiate
8 Bernard Shaw's TV home

10 Disciple
11 Star-crossed lover of Pyramus
12 Power-sharing arrange-ments
15 Salty city in Surrey?
17 Success story's start
20 Work shift
21 A little loopy

25 Musial and Yastrzem-ski's positions: Abbr.
32 Gunslinger at the O.K. Corral
34 Went head-to-head
37 Luster
41 Italian sports car
42 Fails
43 Reed in a pit

46 Some singers
49 Is a pro-prietor
55 Shot in the dark
56 Piece of Arizona terrain
62 Bit of explosive

NORTHEAST
7 Journalist Joseph
14 Gomer of Mayberry
15 Grub

16 Aboriginal Japanese
18 Dr. of rap music
23 From Dixie
24 FICA collector
26 Speakeasy stopper
29 Little nipper
31 The boss, to Hazel
35 Bird life
36 Budget and Alamo rival
39 Big-league lumber
41 Compara-tively bogus
47 Wet blanket
48 Belgian songsmith Jacques
49 Gumbo veggies
50 From the top again
57 Trompe l' __
58 Banquet activities
60 "Sports Center" cable station
61 Flight attendants' walkways
64 One place to order 63 Southeast
65 Impact wetly

wayne robert williams

Professional crossword creator. Home: Florida

Previous Occupations
Art director for a movie magazine, editor-in-chief of a puzzle magazine, author of several books on video games.

Education
High School of Music and Art, attended Hobart College (Geneva, NY).

Crossword Credentials
Created a new line of puzzle magazines for a major publisher. Published several books of his own crosswords, including large-print and cryptics. Edited a revised and expanded version of a popular crossword dictionary, producing typeset pages on a personal computer. Regular contributor to *The New York Times*, *Newsday*, the Crosswords Club, and the Uptown Puzzle Club.

Wayne's artistic background is evident in his crossword diagrams. They all have a distinctively elegant design, with attractive patterns, relatively few black squares, and a larger-than-usual number of theme entries. His diagramless crosswords are known for their unique serpentine shapes.

Like all the top puzzlemakers, Wayne has definite opinions on what types of words should and shouldn't be included in crosswords. His biggest dislike: partial phrases like *Man __ Mancha* for OF LA. He feels such answers detract from a puzzle, and much prefers using an occasional uncommon word.

But one thing is beyond dispute: Wayne puts an extraordinary amount of effort into his crosswords. Once you've completed the four puzzles that follow, you're sure to agree.

Puzzle #37 - "Six Pix"
The ultimate in interlocking themes – every theme answer intersects *three* other theme answers! Wayne had to compile a list of hundreds of 15-letter movie titles to find the six that were used.

Puzzle #38 - "Plenty of Nothing"
A theme executed in an unusual way – partly in the clues, partly in the answers. Note the wide-open "chunks" of letters in each corner of the diagram: 7-by-4 in the upper left and lower right, and 6-by-4 in the upper right and lower left.

Puzzle #39 - "Mealtime"
Perhaps the prettiest diagram of the group, with wide-open areas wherever you look.

Puzzle #40 - "Hidden Clues"
A puzzle with 16 theme-related entries – the eight theme answers *and their clues* are contained within the diagram. An amazing feat of constructing skill!

37
six pix
by wayne robert williams

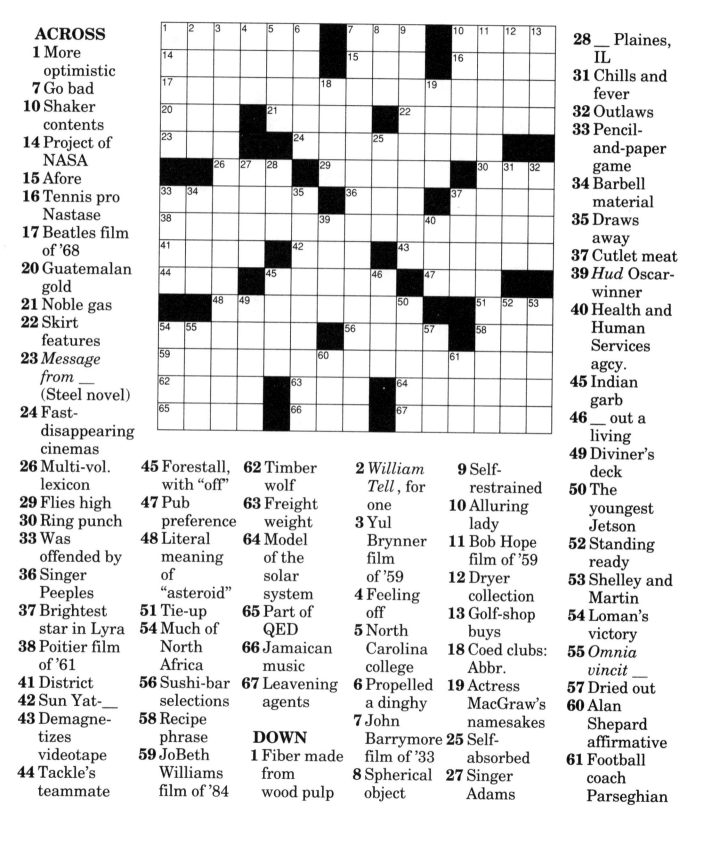

ACROSS
1 More optimistic
7 Go bad
10 Shaker contents
14 Project of NASA
15 Afore
16 Tennis pro Nastase
17 Beatles film of '68
20 Guatemalan gold
21 Noble gas
22 Skirt features
23 *Message from __* (Steel novel)
24 Fast-disappearing cinemas
26 Multi-vol. lexicon
29 Flies high
30 Ring punch
33 Was offended by
36 Singer Peeples
37 Brightest star in Lyra
38 Poitier film of '61
41 District
42 Sun Yat-__
43 Demagne-tizes videotape
44 Tackle's teammate

45 Forestall, with "off"
47 Pub preference
48 Literal meaning of "asteroid"
51 Tie-up
54 Much of North Africa
56 Sushi-bar selections
58 Recipe phrase
59 JoBeth Williams film of '84

62 Timber wolf
63 Freight weight
64 Model of the solar system
65 Part of QED
66 Jamaican music
67 Leavening agents

DOWN
1 Fiber made from wood pulp

2 *William Tell*, for one
3 Yul Brynner film of '59
4 Feeling off
5 North Carolina college
6 Propelled a dinghy
7 John Barrymore film of '33
8 Spherical object

9 Self-restrained
10 Alluring lady
11 Bob Hope film of '59
12 Dryer collection
13 Golf-shop buys
18 Coed clubs: Abbr.
19 Actress MacGraw's namesakes
25 Self-absorbed
27 Singer Adams

28 __ Plaines, IL
31 Chills and fever
32 Outlaws
33 Pencil-and-paper game
34 Barbell material
35 Draws away
37 Cutlet meat
39 *Hud* Oscar-winner
40 Health and Human Services agcy.
45 Indian garb
46 __ out a living
49 Diviner's deck
50 The youngest Jetson
52 Standing ready
53 Shelley and Martin
54 Loman's victory
55 *Omnia vincit __*
57 Dried out
60 Alan Shepard affirmative
61 Football coach Parseghian

38
plenty of nothing
by wayne robert williams

ACROSS

1 Driver's license ritual
8 Tidal movements
12 Altar vows
16 Lamarr role in a '49 film
17 Political suffix
18 *And Then There Were __*
19 Lightweight cotton fabric
20 Meeting place
21 California alternative
22 TV zip
24 Newspaper notice
25 Followed
26 Finnish architect
27 Complete collections
31 Equator's latitude
34 Noble Brit
37 Surpass
38 Contributory cause
39 Astrologer Sydney
42 An NCO
45 Prov. clock setting
46 OO-
49 Pasture eater
50 Gather in
52 Upbeat, in music
53 Nettles
55 Word form for "skull"
57 Coin
58 *Lawrence of Arabia* star
64 Dancer Pavlova
65 Chew the scenery
66 Starr reporter
69 Pentathlon need
70 0-0
76 One manipulated
77 Younger brother
78 Crying
79 Ivy League team
80 Siberian river
81 Like romantic nights
82 Actress Russo
83 Too curious
84 Tex-Mex choice

DOWN

1 Churchill successor
2 Subject of Himalayan legends
3 Lively enthusiasm
4 Appropriate moment
5 *Middlemarch* author
6 Part of many California town names
7 Broadway version of a Baum classic
8 Parrot, e.g.
9 *One-Eyed Jacks* director
10 Big bundle
11 Embattled town of 7/44
12 Some boat motors
13 Bond
14 Like some inspections
15 Brief bouts
23 Comic Olsen
26 Star's rep.
27 *60 Minutes* reporter
28 Wipe clean
29 O O O
30 Mach 2 flier
32 Village, to Wilhelm
33 Violent straits
35 Little piggie
36 Anatomist's prefix
39 Saturn's wife
40 Med. scanning technology
41 Monogram of a 50's candidate
43 Oscar-winner as Kris Kringle
44 Seed coat
47 Spunk
48 Alien word form
51 Make-believe
54 *Green Acres* name
56 "All the Things You __"
58 Kind of frog
59 Pierce
60 Old French coin
61 Solar-system model
62 Founder of the American Shakers
63 Join up
67 Prefix for surgical
68 Namesakes of a whodunit dog
70 Picture-copying method
71 See 75 Down
72 Spanish muralist
73 Western Samoa money
74 Family of the crocus and gladiolus
75 Word frequently following 71 Down

39
mealtime
by wayne robert williams

ACROSS

1 British candies
8 Furlough
13 Nickel-and-__ (petty sort)
18 Island strings
19 Opening Day time
20 M. Zola
21 Capote classic
24 Lip protector
25 Coat fur
26 Surrender by deed
27 Part of an apron
30 Considerate
31 __ Lingus
32 French wine
33 Peter Weller film of '91
37 Sleeve cards
38 Devour
39 Linguist's suffix
40 *Foreign Affairs* author
41 Doesn't play it straight
42 Fish-eating birds
43 Soap shape
44 Work unit
45 Has second thoughts
47 Russian river
49 Rolling Stones album of '68
55 Played an Elizabethan instrument
57 Skirt design
58 *I Remember Mama* mama
59 Hemingway memoir
64 This: Sp.
65 Heckart and Brennan
66 Pan-American Union successor: Abbr.
68 "__ the season . . ."

69 Sales target
72 Public-education pioneer
73 Fly apart
75 50 Down, for example
76 Operate
77 "__ Lama Ding Dong" ('61 tune)
78 Da Vinci subject
80 Addams Family member
81 Typesetter's widths
82 __ Ogai (important Japanese novelist)
83 *A Chorus Line* finale

84 Liquid part of blood
86 Colorful wrap
88 Down with: Fr.
92 Peter Weir film of '75
96 Nicknames for Arden namesakes
97 One of the Osmonds
98 Water passage
99 Counsels, in Kent
100 Nottingham's river
101 Had a secret rendezvous

DOWN

1 Country-music great Ernest
2 Gumbo ingredient

3 Combustibles
4 One way to serve steak
5 Mouse-spotter's cry
6 Subordinate Claus
7 Actress Young
8 Open framework
9 Eastern Orthodox bishop
10 Bandleader Shaw
11 Résumé, for short
12 Samuel's mentor
13 Tables
14 Ayatollah's title
15 Garson's Oscar role

16 Blissful
17 Takes offense
22 Moslem sect
23 South African bulb
28 Having an off day
29 Book-jacket copy
31 Sour-tasting
33 Science fiction award
34 Ginger root
35 Word form for "horn"
36 Exhort
37 Nautical rescue system
41 *Bonanza* name
42 Humor conclusion
45 Very thin fashion models
46 Outermost point

48 Relative rank
50 From which you may get the lead out
51 *The Right Stuff* character
52 Pull the plug on
53 Whole
54 Coming-attractions ad, e.g.
56 "Agnus __"
60 Where to find Richard Saunders' byline
61 Smiles expansively
62 Classify
63 Renaissance poet
67 Dumbfound
69 Cleat, for instance
70 Last longer than
71 Heartburn relief
73 Title for Elgar or Lipton
74 Calling into play
77 Negligent
78 Cleveland suburb
79 Nuggets of wisdom
82 Slalom gold-medalist in '84
85 Cut, old-style
86 Gravitational force
87 Essence
89 Gravy holder
90 Teen trauma
91 Choo-choo listing
93 Qty.
94 Suffix for part
95 *The __ Divorcee* (Astaire/Rogers film)

40

hidden clues

by wayne robert williams

ACROSS

1 Semitic goddess
8 Part of a Muslim palace
13 *Jacqueline __ Once Is Not Enough* ('75 film)
20 Most overused
21 Have __ in (be part of)
22 Castaway's clan
23 Clue for 94 Down
25 Spin over and over
26 Irish county
27 Tony-winner Hagen
28 New Deal org.
30 Idyllic spots
31 Awaiting an heir, as Henry VIII
34 Needle case
35 Hurler Hershiser
36 Clue for 33 Down
40 Letter opener
43 Architectural style
46 Hear a case again
47 Brit's raincoat
49 Fit words to music
50 Ladd and Shepard
51 Refuses to sign, in a way
53 Magellan's successor
54 La-la lead-in
55 Sportscaster Gowdy
56 Prefix for port
57 Kind of camera, initially
58 Iranian belief
60 Grand Teton beast
61 Clue for 18 Down
65 Make better
66 Uninteresting
68 Concert site
69 Speak indistinctly
70 Kind of energy
72 Clue for 12 Down
74 Caribbean colony: Abbr.
77 Despicable sort

78 Give, as odds
79 __ Penh
80 Grandpa on *The Waltons*
81 Pindar piece
82 *The Unbearable Lightness of Being* star
84 Founding family of an upstate New York city
87 Grand Canyon transport
88 Liveliness
89 Dundee denial
90 Bolivian lake
91 City near New Bedford
93 Clapton of rock
95 Clue for 76 Down
98 See 17 Down
100 __ *Make a Deal*

101 Building builder
104 Contemptuous exclamation
106 Adjective suffix
107 Empty words
109 Humble dwelling
111 Poker openers, perhaps
114 Clue for 61 Down
118 Frank quality
119 Strong dislike
120 Becomes gloomy
121 Czech Republic city
122 Has the appearance of
123 Polaris, Trident or Atlas

DOWN
1 Dangerous snakes
2 Convertiplanes

3 Revenge, to Nero
4 Service-station job
5 Dyes
6 Mao __-tung
7 DDE arena
8 Sword handle
9 Peerce performance
10 Fox-network sitcom
11 Members of a certain college
12 See 72 Across
13 CRT display
14 Press finish
15 Apartment-house employee
16 Digressive comments
17 Clue for 98 Across
18 See 61 Across
19 Aerospatiale products

24 Melt together
29 About, for short
32 __ Marie Saint
33 See 36 Across
34 Diminutive ending
35 __ upswing (rising)
37 Creative flair
38 Corp. boss
39 Horoscope writer Sydney
41 Played again
42 Not at all flighty
43 Turn toward
44 Hebrew month
45 Clue for 48 Down
48 See 45 Down
52 Blissful
53 Noisy
56 Letters on '68 campaign buttons
57 Man of clay?
59 __ Darya (Asian river)

61 See 114 Across
62 Spanish article
63 Summer hrs in SC
64 Criticize harshly
67 Hasty escape
69 Part of the school yr.
70 Purview
71 The Cistercians, e.g.
72 Circular
73 Pater __
75 __ Beach, FL
76 See 95 Across
80 Rifle parts
83 Sgt. Friday's employer
84 Last movement, in music
85 Skippers keep them
86 Org. for Dr. Joyce Brothers
87 Sausage grinders
90 Pretenders, old-style
92 Frequent *Wheel of Fortune* purchase
94 See 23 Across
96 Keebler cookiemaker
97 Hallucinogen, for short
99 Tibetan for "holy land"
102 Convex moldings
103 Chase away
104 Jolly laughs
105 Some: Sp.
107 Woebegone
108 Uses a sight
110 Dissolve, as bacteria
112 BBC rival
113 Shaggy Scandinavian rug
115 Crusty dessert
116 Rickover's rank: Abbr.
117 Skater Babilonia

eric albert

Professional crossword creator. Home: Massachusetts

Previous Occupations
Computer scientist, interpreter for the deaf, psychotherapist.

Education
B.A. in computer science from Brown University, M.A. in counseling psychology from Lesley College (Cambridge, MA).

Crossword Credentials
Creator of the first artificial intelligence computer program that constructs top-quality crosswords. Creator of the crossword in the *Nikkei Weekly* (an English-language newspaper based in Tokyo). Creates intricate contest crosswords for a major puzzle magazine.

While crossword software for the personal computer has been around for a number of years, its practical applications have been limited to puzzle-solving and editorial housekeeping. There have been a few crossword-making programs, but they produce very primitive puzzles that are based on a small word list and filled with unusual words and crosswordese.

Eric Albert has changed all that. He has "taught" his computer not only how to create crosswords, but how to use the best possible words in doing so. The key to the system is his massive database of 750,000 words and phrases. Eric's ongoing project is to give a quality ranking to each database entry; so far, he's completed all the entries of eight letters or less, or about one-third of the total. Using this procedure, CBS NEWS, for example, ranks very high, while ANOA is at the opposite end of the scale. The computer doesn't do it all – Eric still creates the diagrams and the clues. The clues, once written, go into a database of their own.

Eric's puzzles bring to mind an interesting philosophical question: Are these puzzles Eric's work, or his computer's? Make no mistake – Eric has done all the work (thousands of hours worth); his computer is only a high-tech tool that carries out his instructions. Thanks to Eric, we're getting a tantalizing glimpse of what the next generation of crosswords will be like.

Puzzle #41 - "Themeless"
The 6-by-5 corners (in the upper left and lower right) are a rarity for human constructors, and are even tougher to do using only common words. But Eric's computer program *prefers* working with wide-open isolated corners. The variety of names, phrases, and lively language herein attests to the success of his database-rating efforts.

Puzzle #42 - "Just Teasing"
This puzzle and #43 show how Eric's program can create puzzles with special restrictions. In this case: using a certain letter of the alphabet as often as possible. Thirty percent of the boxes you'll fill in will contain the same letter!

Puzzle #43 - "Once Is Enough"
A very tricky theme, opposite in character (sort of) from #42. You may have trouble making your answers fit until you figure out what's going on.

Puzzle #44 - "Spelling It Out"
Crossword fans have to be good spellers, right? So you'll have no difficulty here. With interesting nontheme phrases throughout, this is another showcase for Eric's database.

41
themeless
by eric albert

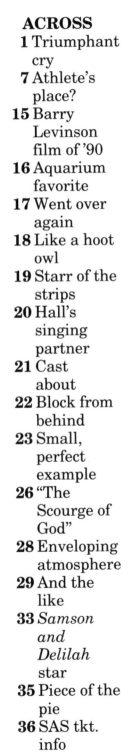

ACROSS
1 Triumphant cry
7 Athlete's place?
15 Barry Levinson film of '90
16 Aquarium favorite
17 Went over again
18 Like a hoot owl
19 Starr of the strips
20 Hall's singing partner
21 Cast about
22 Block from behind
23 Small, perfect example
26 "The Scourge of God"
28 Enveloping atmosphere
29 And the like
33 *Samson and Delilah* star
35 Piece of the pie
36 SAS tkt. info

38 Crude quarters
39 Madam, in Málaga
41 Legendary gold-laden land
43 Brest friends
44 Black-hat wearer
46 So far
47 Parking-garage feature
48 Library area

53 Bannister, notably
54 One in bondage
55 Robert De Niro role
58 Where films must "play"
59 Volume units?
60 Italian designer
61 Kitten quality
62 Put straight

DOWN
1 Puts clothes on
2 Out in the open
3 Spud
4 Genetic duplicate
5 Be defensible
6 Pace for Pavarotti
7 Name in the news
8 Bring to mind

9 Warlike
10 Parakeet's cry
11 Makes a bed, maybe
12 Follow the rainbow
13 Comedian Kabibble
14 Curious George's creator
23 Tropical treat
24 Botched one

25 Mrs. Donahue
27 One more than *due*
28 *Omnia vincit __*
29 English assignment
30 English assignment
31 "Pipe down!"
32 Youngest of the gods
34 Marine greeting
37 Math subj.
40 Seafood order
42 Cleaning receptacle
45 Makes modifications to
47 Become mature
49 Bouquet
50 Diamond measure
51 *A Fish Called Wanda* actor
52 Done in
53 Put together
55 Letters of introduction?
56 "Skip to My __"
57 Barracks bed

42

just teasing

by eric albert

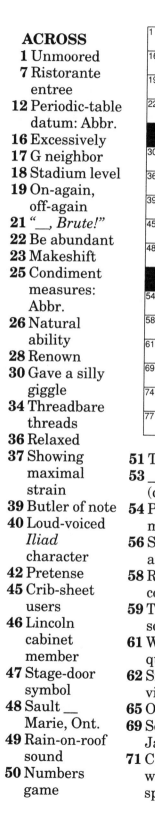

ACROSS

1 Unmoored
7 Ristorante entree
12 Periodic-table datum: Abbr.
16 Excessively
17 G neighbor
18 Stadium level
19 On-again, off-again
21 "__, *Brute!*"
22 Be abundant
23 Makeshift
25 Condiment measures: Abbr.
26 Natural ability
28 Renown
30 Gave a silly giggle
34 Threadbare threads
36 Relaxed
37 Showing maximal strain
39 Butler of note
40 Loud-voiced *Iliad* character
42 Pretense
45 Crib-sheet users
46 Lincoln cabinet member
47 Stage-door symbol
48 Sault __ Marie, Ont.
49 Rain-on-roof sound
50 Numbers game

51 Takes turns
53 __ water (cologne)
54 Put into motion
56 Speaks like a sparrow
58 Rorschach's concerns
59 Thoughtless sort
61 Write quickly
62 Small villages
65 Overlenient
69 Soul-singer James
71 Commune with spirits?

74 Atkins of country music
75 Make reparations
76 Precisely
77 Course length
78 Saxophone range
79 "__ Girl" (Billy Joel tune)

DOWN

1 Go __ (fight)
2 Completely cooked
3 Fixed routine

4 Bit of news
5 In favor of
6 Piper's son
7 Touched on the head
8 Burns' flower
9 Caught some Z's
10 Sharp flavor
11 "__ girl!"
12 Put away
13 Gossip
14 Rec-room fixture
15 Has faith in
20 Gilligan's home

24 He built Russia a "window to the West"
26 It's held for questioning
27 "You __ So Beautiful"
29 Dol. fractions
30 Mini-pies
31 *Some Like* __
32 Playground piece
33 Makes lace
34 Individual instructor
35 Like __ of bricks
37 Bivouac sights

38 Start stud
40 Body politic
41 London gallery
43 Handle the food for
44 Goes jogging
46 Tiff
47 *And __ Goes* (Ellerbee book)
49 Hiding place
50 Mississippi pol Trent
52 Retired, to Nolan Ryan
53 "__ the season . . ."
54 Hopeless
55 Cover, in a way
56 Not this one, old-style
57 In the know
59 Rock star John
60 "I __ kick from champagne"
63 At the drop of __
64 Small sum
65 RBI, for example
66 *Beetle Bailey* dog
67 Went by quickly
68 Bobbysoxer, e.g.
70 Off-hrs. cash source
72 A/C unit
73 Alley follower

43

once is enough

by eric albert

ACROSS

1 Successful, on Broadway
5 Changeless
13 Soprano's note
18 Similar
19 Bargain successfully, in a way
20 Easter ritual
21 *The Rose Tattoo* writer
23 Popular Mouseketeer
24 Worn-out
25 *Buck Privates* star
26 Needle droppers
27 Most massive living thing
29 Preview a film
31 Midafternoon
32 "The Tears __ Clown" (#1 tune of '70)
33 Bridges in Hollywood
34 Monteverdi opera
37 Dallas sch.
40 *Searching for Bobby Fischer* game
42 Powerful business-person
43 Yanks' home
46 Drivel
47 Gab
50 Bear's advice
51 Balance center
53 Computer accessory
54 "I coulda __ contender"
55 Lose on purpose
56 Yanks' home
58 Happen to
59 Turkey of a show
60 Pirate's pet

62 Almond-flavored liqueur
64 Three-time ring king
65 Wharton, for one
68 Masked mammal
69 Conducted
70 Harriet's husband
71 Party giver
72 Kite nemesis
73 Catches cattle
75 Do
77 Mischievous kid
80 Mindless followers
82 Bottle part
83 Jaguar rival

87 Walter Scott heroine
89 Actress Skye
90 Sheer fear
91 Loads and loads
92 Legislative subgroup
97 Finish second
98 Literally, "small armored one"
99 Tied
100 Toady's responses
101 Never-ending
102 Blacksmith-turned-inventor

DOWN

1 Man in a box

2 Stieglitz's spouse
3 Fishy?
4 Boxer's combo
5 Skating surface
6 Hayloft
7 News source: Abbr.
8 Skyscraping
9 Where the bees are
10 Let slip
11 *The Apartment* star
12 Right on a map
13 Bucket of bolts
14 Touch off
15 Global-warming mechanism

16 Owl, often
17 Monty Python member
22 Throw a bon-voyage party
28 Brezhnev bungalow
29 Freezing rain
30 Blackjack, in Britain
34 Emulates the Blob
35 Level to the ground
36 Attention-getting ad word
37 Banned pitch
38 Sewer access
39 Economic segment
41 Not vert.
42 Key point

44 Bradley or Boxer
45 Solo
47 Put in stitches
48 Melodramatize
49 Beethoven's hometown
52 Plunder
54 Ballpark brew
56 Imported cheese
57 *The Paper* director Howard
58 False god
60 *The Godfather* author
61 Working-or-not
62 Sounds of pleasure
63 Repeated figure, in music
65 Head honcho
66 Auctioneer's confederate
67 Light brown
74 Each
75 Pix biz
76 Oratorio relatives
78 Copycat's remark
79 Doctor-to-be's major
80 Mighty untidy
81 Grid group
82 __ Dame
84 Make it
85 Cad
86 Sherlock's love
88 Put a value on
89 Singer who won the Nobel prize
93 __ *fixe*
94 Bubkes
95 Unrestrained joy
96 Whispers sweet nothings

44
spelling it out
by eric albert

ACROSS

1 Jazz saxophonist Zoot
5 Ancient Mariner's burden
14 Painting backing
20 Do needle work
21 Lump in one's throat?
22 The Far East
23 Letters on love letters
25 Stand in the way of
26 Bad-mouth, in current parlance
27 Took a stroll
28 Lummox
30 Poker holding
31 USN officer
32 Meets with
33 Evil demon
36 Sigourney Weaver sci-fi thriller
37 Cul-de-sac
39 Of a dull gray
41 Gentleman's gentleman
43 A Day in Hollywood
44 Wage slave's exclamation
46 Collapsible bed
49 *The Joy __ Club*
50 Like knit fabrics
52 Put in order
53 King Mongkut subject
54 Ordinal suffix
55 Flim-flam
56 Dunderhead
57 Hero of a '36 novel
58 Diaphanous
59 Not well done
61 Bit of a bite
62 Chant in a '50s kids series
68 Iroquois League member
69 Sargasso Sea dwellers
70 Parson's quarters
71 cummings creations
72 Airy thing
74 *Carmen* composer
75 Kernel holder

78 Course hazard
79 Long-lasting wave
80 Western item
82 Tip one's hat
83 "__ darn tootin'!"
84 Ma Bell
86 Covers with sod
87 A-C-E, e.g.
89 Billions of years
90 Take it easy
92 Scintillate
94 Bugs' pursuer
96 Yawn-provoking
97 Chou En-__
98 Strong-smelling
99 *Star Trek: Deep Space Nine* character
100 __ *Spirit* (Coward comedy)
102 LBJ successor

103 Whenever one wishes
105 Film rating
110 Gym class
111 Mall mover
112 *The Way We __*
113 Giggle
114 Halt suddenly
115 Nowhere near

DOWN

1 Head for the hills
2 How to wash socks
3 40 Down, formally
4 Criterion: Abbr.
5 Smarts
6 Hit a high ball
7 Jordan's former team
8 *The African Queen* scriptwriter

9 Safe-hits-pavement sound
10 Vitamin-bottle stat.
11 Mork's home
12 "__ wise guy, eh?"
13 Watch through a keyhole
14 Salon job
15 Throwing ability
16 Valve-joining pipe
17 Beta alternative
18 Actress MacDowell
19 Star, in Stuttgart
24 Watering holes
29 Very, often
33 Stick-in-the-mud
34 D-Day nickname

35 Unsightly sight
36 Campaign '36 name
38 Cartoonist Browne
39 Transported
40 A Little Woman
42 Nautical direction
44 Jeweled headdress
45 Top grade
47 *Them* author
48 Name on the cover
50 Chutzpah
51 Onion cousin
53 "__ Coins in the Fountain"
55 Considers, with "on"
56 Bobbysoxers' concerns
57 Drive out
58 Ne'er-do-well
59 Slightest sound

60 Fly-by-night operator?
61 Renoir contemporary
62 Use up
63 Pulitzer Prize poet
64 Empire State bumper sticker
65 Polite assent
66 Nellie Forbush's love
67 Formal-garden feature of old
72 Did garden work
73 Wrath
74 Queen's subjects
75 Snorkeling site
76 Behind the scenes, in a way
77 Big name in behaviorism
79 Cake-sale sponsor
80 Redolence
81 Washington or Whitney: Abbr.
82 Coin a nickname
84 Objective
85 Billie Jean King, __ Moffitt
86 President with 15 children
88 Dashing
90 Superman's archenemy
91 Man with a horn
92 *USA Today* illustration
93 Metal-shop machine
95 Takes easy strides
96 "I feel the same way"
99 Shoppe-signe worde
100 Loudness units
101 Rachel's sister
104 Atticus Finch's creator
106 VMI clock setting
107 *Foucault's Pendulum* author
108 Wide divergence
109 Frequent flier

merl reagle

Professional crossword creator. Home: Florida

Previous Occupations
Newspaper copy editor, rock keyboardist, screenwriter, TV game-show writer.

Education
Attended the University of Arizona.

Crossword Credentials
Creator of the Sunday crossword in the *San Francisco Examiner* since 1985. Directed the only major crossword tournament ever held west of the Mississippi (Los Angeles, 1985). Created a puzzle celebrating the 75th anniversary of crosswords for *LIFE* magazine (1988).

Merl Reagle's crosswords are noteworthy for their wide-open diagrams and outrageous humor, the roots of which can be found in his childhood. He was a big fan of the fast, clever gags in Warner Bros. cartoons (and still does a great Elmer Fudd impersonation). Merl is the youngest person to have a crossword published in *The New York Times*. Margaret Farrar published Merl's first *New York Times* puzzle, a harbinger of things to come, when he was 15. It had three 15-letter answers across the middle (ALEUTIAN ISLANDS, STATE OF THE UNION, and SALES RESISTANCE) and one down the center (INNOCENTS ABROAD) for good measure!

Merl is the crossword world's most successful self-publisher, having sold tens of thousands of copies of his puzzle collections from the *San Francisco Examiner*. He was one of the first puzzle professionals to publicly advocate that crosswords be more reflective of contemporary life. His willingness to speak out on the subject, when few others were doing so, helped lay the groundwork for the "puzzling renaissance" that is taking place today.

Puzzle #45 - "Cornering Ability"
A themeless puzzle that makes for a fascinating contrast with Eric Albert's #41. Both are remarkably wide-open (including extra-chunky corners), and both have a nice variety of words. Who do *you* think does the "better" job – man or computer?

Puzzle #46 - "Optical Allusions"
Whenever a crossword has less than one-sixth of the total squares black, you can be sure that the constructor has put a lot of extra effort into it. Crosswords this size (17x17) average about 48 black squares, but this one has only 39! That means a more challenging interlock, with more long words than usual.

Puzzle #47 - "Russian Capitalism"
Suggested names for some of the new businesses opening up over there.

Puzzle #48 - "First Addition"
All of the twelve theme answers either intersect or are adjacent to at least one other theme answer. Remarkably, *nine* of them intersect 25 Down!

45
cornering ability
by merl reagle

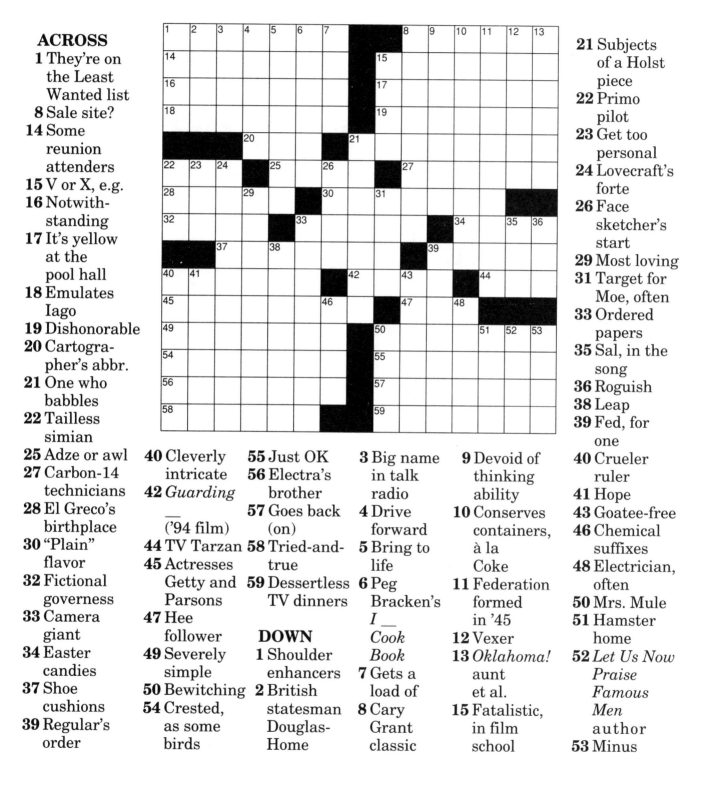

ACROSS
1 They're on the Least Wanted list
8 Sale site?
14 Some reunion attenders
15 V or X, e.g.
16 Notwithstanding
17 It's yellow at the pool hall
18 Emulates Iago
19 Dishonorable
20 Cartographer's abbr.
21 One who babbles
22 Tailless simian
25 Adze or awl
27 Carbon-14 technicians
28 El Greco's birthplace
30 "Plain" flavor
32 Fictional governess
33 Camera giant
34 Easter candies
37 Shoe cushions
39 Regular's order
40 Cleverly intricate
42 *Guarding* __ ('94 film)
44 TV Tarzan
45 Actresses Getty and Parsons
47 Hee follower
49 Severely simple
50 Bewitching
54 Crested, as some birds
55 Just OK
56 Electra's brother
57 Goes back (on)
58 Tried-and-true
59 Dessertless TV dinners

DOWN
1 Shoulder enhancers
2 British statesman Douglas-Home
3 Big name in talk radio
4 Drive forward
5 Bring to life
6 Peg Bracken's *I __ Cook Book*
7 Gets a load of
8 Cary Grant classic
9 Devoid of thinking ability
10 Conserves containers, à la Coke
11 Federation formed in '45
12 Vexer
13 *Oklahoma!* aunt et al.
15 Fatalistic, in film school
21 Subjects of a Holst piece
22 Primo pilot
23 Get too personal
24 Lovecraft's forte
26 Face sketcher's start
29 Most loving
31 Target for Moe, often
33 Ordered papers
35 Sal, in the song
36 Roguish
38 Leap
39 Fed, for one
40 Crueler ruler
41 Hope
43 Goatee-free
46 Chemical suffixes
48 Electrician, often
50 Mrs. Mule
51 Hamster home
52 *Let Us Now Praise Famous Men* author
53 Minus

46
optical allusions
by merl reagle

ACROSS
1 Footballer-turned-actor
11 Clavell bestseller
17 Hollywood-lunch agendas
18 Trinidad's sister
19 '72 tune written by Springsteen
21 Diminutive suffix
22 Place with a checkout counter: Abbr.
23 Electronics giant
24 Ship's hdg.
25 And that kind of thing: Abbr.
26 Sponsorship
28 Stock-market stats
30 Composer Saint-__
32 Salty dogs
34 Lost
38 Piedmont region
41 Circulated
43 Jackson Browne tune of '73
47 Mosquito milieu
48 *The Name of the Rose* author
49 Guitar device
50 Where London Br. is now
52 Parma pronoun

53 Arthur's namesakes
55 Foreigner tune of '78
58 Bronx cheer
60 "Jolly Good Fellow" verb
61 Conductor Dorati
62 Got set on 18
64 Tennis surface
68 Where to find Today's Special
70 Brogan bottoms
73 Handbag hue
74 Joyful dance

53 Arthur's namesakes
55 Foreigner tune of '78
58 Bronx cheer
60 "Jolly Good Fellow" verb
61 Conductor Dorati
62 Got set on 18
64 Tennis surface
68 Where to find Today's Special
70 Brogan bottoms
73 Handbag hue
74 Joyful dance

77 Brotherly brood
79 Actress Caldwell
80 Southwestern tie
81 '72 Johnny Nash tune
85 Mr. Gulliver
86 Roz role
87 Economist's observations
88 Unkempt

DOWN
1 Walks without care
2 Dolores Haze, familiarly
3 Make manifest

4 PED __ (street sign)
5 One sneaker?
6 *Die Fledermaus* role
7 Excavate anew
8 Roger the toon
9 __ Khan
10 Planes costing $50 mil.
11 Office skill
12 Jihad
13 Ginza belt
14 Redcoat general
15 Chorus of disgust

16 Pay particular attention to
20 In its place, as a .38
26 Part of NAACP
27 Cooking herb
29 Cool it
31 Rebel Turner
33 Fit for a king
35 Word on Finnish coins
36 Film composer Morricone
37 Extra
39 NAFTA concern
40 Entreat repeatedly
42 "__ said many times . . ."

43 John's *Urban Cowboy* costar
44 Where shells come from
45 Where shells end up
46 __ *Only Old Once* (Dr. Seuss book)
51 Criticizes sharply
54 Hormel bestseller
56 Off-weeks, in sports
57 Leb. neighbor
59 Like the meek
63 Donut purchases
65 Keyless, as music
66 Strauss opera
67 Fooled completely
69 Seasonal songs
71 Averse
72 Creepy
74 Leave in the lurch
75 Cake finisher
76 Ready to take a chance
78 Large amount
80 "You want to run that __ again?"
82 She's taken a vow
83 Him: Fr.
84 Trotsky's given name

47
russian capitalism
by merl reagle

ACROSS

1 Post-punchline question
6 Capacitance unit
11 *La __* ('54 Fellini film)
17 Sneezin's greeting
18 Forget-me-not's family
19 *With a Song in My Heart* subject
20 Russian nightclub?
22 Galileo and his neighbors
23 Ring results
24 Synagogue pointer
25 Russian informal restaurant?
27 Welsh pooch
29 Naval agreement
30 Recruit's status
31 Goya's duchess
34 Undersized
37 Clinch
39 Russian children's store?
42 Fantasy-world creator
47 Bovine, to a tot
48 A place to spend guilders
51 Angelic glow
52 Paradoxical question, in Zen
53 Russian hat store?
55 Sci-fi author Stanislaw
56 Italian director Petri
58 Zip, to Zola
59 Jet hotshot
60 Russian comedy club?
65 Spanish muralist

67 Michael Douglas' dad
68 Hearing-aid company
69 Counterpart of Eos
71 Confidential, as information
73 Russian hospitality house?
75 Grad
78 Comes face-to-face with
79 The Mennonites, for instance
80 Sincere
83 Loser at Vicksburg
85 Heroine of an 1869 novel
87 Russian jazz club?

91 Gun-owner's grp.
92 911 responder
95 Busy __
96 Russian kennel?
99 Say no to
100 Traveled by roadster
101 Had in mind
102 Musberger and Scowcroft
103 Have a little salmon?
104 "__ the Lord my soul . . ."

DOWN

1 Stare stupidly
2 Recording-studio effect
3 "Memories Are Made of __"
4 Yellow moths

5 Home of Komazawa Olympic Park
6 London creeper
7 ". . . and pretty maids all in __"
8 Sitar selection
9 Greek shopping place
10 Bad news for commuters
11 Dirty Harry's employer: Abbr.
12 "Marine Hymn" place
13 Violin-bow application
14 Stun
15 *Taxi* costar
16 Anatomical loop

18 Villain
21 Peter of Peter, Paul and Mary
26 Society-page word
27 *Julius Caesar* plotter
28 Not playing hooky
31 Bucks dispenser: Abbr.
32 Checked (on)
33 They may be late
35 Constant
36 Dr. Zhivago
38 Sun-dried brick
40 Hearing-test components
41 Drop
43 __ Na Na
44 *The Guns of __* ('61 action film)

45 Super-exciting
46 Yesteryear
49 Up a tree
50 Indy winner Luyendyk
53 Buster Brown's dog
54 Come next
55 Norse troublemaker
57 Envelope sticker
61 Emulate Killy
62 Like NASDAQ trading
63 Adverse fate
64 "This round's __!" (sport's words)
66 Unevenly worn
69 Gather on a surface, in chemistry
70 Tiny toiler
72 Most moist
74 Made up (for)
76 Fail finale
77 Peach __ (desserts)
80 Bremen's river
81 Dishonor
82 PBS newscaster MacNeil
84 Try to corner the market
86 Wynonna's mom
87 Zinger
88 Tahoe transactions
89 "__ move on!"
90 Take __ (acknowledge applause)
92 Nicholas or Alexander
93 Lady Chaplin
94 Feel for
97 Nikkei Exchange currency
98 Agent, for short

48

first addition

by merl reagle

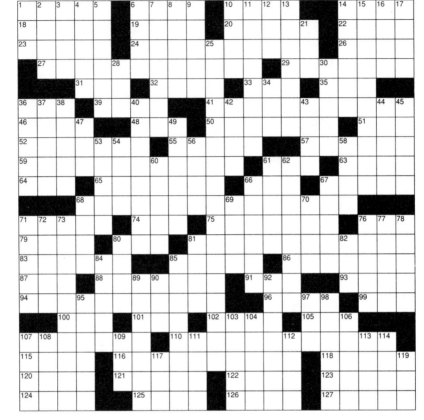

ACROSS
1 Extra
6 PD alerts
10 Western Indians
14 Does not exist
18 Sport of eight-second rides
19 Prepare presents
20 Out of __ (cranky)
22 NIT rival
23 Oppenheimer project
24 Bouquet billionaire?
26 Not quite dry
27 Out-of-shape singer?
29 Takes on again
31 Rim attachment
32 Latch __
33 A day in Acapulco
35 Ending for access
36 Plastic product
39 "Watch your head!"
41 Actor's exclusive establishment?
46 City south of Lillehammer
48 Exhaustive word ref.
50 Redenbacher jarful
51 Cytoplasm material
52 Gatecrasher
55 Game authority
57 Close-by
59 Bellyaching bandleader?
61 Grain beard
63 Mussel genus
64 On everybody's buy list
65 Author
66 Clark's *Mogambo* costar
67 Copper's bopper
68 Noted novelist?
71 Arthurian sorceress
74 Not any, in law
75 Old bucket of bolts
76 Grate stuff

79 Tile color
80 Orthography contest
81 Macho anchorman?
83 Drudge
85 Drudge
86 Diminutive bone
87 Diminutive ending
88 "E-I-E-I-O" is one
91 Poorly lit
93 Complain
94 Singer's son who loves cars?
96 Pickoff throws
99 "So *that's* it!"
100 Fistic Muslim
101 $C_{20}H_{25}N_3O$
102 *Bridges of Madison County* state

105 Make a move
107 Like some wieners
110 Trickster talk-show host?
115 City near Mauna Loa
116 Software magnate who invests conservatively?
118 Florida flier
120 "__ to that, brother!"
121 East African tribe
122 Verne character
123 See 93 Across
124 M's main man
125 Rhett's last word
126 Some retirement capital
127 Hero's horse

DOWN
1 Angelico, for one
2 Name in Virginia politics
3 Thing of worship
4 Drop flavor
5 Threw easily
6 Out of whack
7 Antagonize
8 Area drained by a river
9 Used up
10 Mail letters?
11 "I must have patience __ the load": Shak.
12 Reckon wrongly
13 Warehouse's purpose
14 Nehru's daughter
15 Horror-film actor?

16 Tag info
17 A little night music
21 Sault __ Marie, Ont.
25 Actress at the Cow Palace?
28 Heat unit, familiarly
30 British composer Gustav
34 King __ Saud
36 *Garden of Earthly Delights* artist
37 The Jetsons' dog
38 Crow
40 *The Godfather* family name
42 Charles II's portraitist
43 __ Bator
44 *Bugsy* scorer Morricone
45 Densest gas
47 Sphere
49 *Maître __*

53 *Enterprise* doc
54 Work to get
56 "Alas!"
58 '50s Red-hunting panel: Abbr.
60 Lash of westerns
61 __-garde
62 Return on foot
66 Mistreated
67 Tractor garages
68 Tractor-trailer job
69 "Welcome to" sign abbr.
70 Thunderbolt thrower
71 "__ pray"
72 *Salle de classe* place
73 Rotgut-loving radio personality?
76 U.S. metals giant
77 Psalms word
78 African scavenger
80 Tunesmith Jacques
81 Muse of history
82 Allen of *Home Improvement*
84 Cartoonist Bushmiller
85 Certain bivalve
89 Had regrets
90 Hosp. professionals
92 Rio beach
95 Ice-cream flavoring
97 Natter
98 Pressure, metaphorically
103 Muscat native
104 Desert's dearth
106 Close-fitting
107 Single-minded seaman
108 Prom Night wheels
109 Pressure unit: Abbr.
111 Acting Ken or Lena
112 Bears: Sp.
113 Toledo's lake
114 Hawaiian goose
117 *The Heart __ Lonely Hunter*
119 Jane Fonda's hubby

will shortz

Puzzle editor of The New York Times. *Home: New York*

Previous Occupation
Editor-in-Chief, *Games* magazine.

Education
B.A. in enigmatology from Indiana University, law degree from the University of Virginia.

Crossword Credentials
See below.

"He was born to be crossword editor of *The New York Times.*" So said Jack Rosenthal, Will's boss at the *Times*, in an interview soon after the beginning of its "Shortz Era." Quite literally, Will's entire life has been devoted to puzzles.

As a child, Will had joked to friends about getting a college major in puzzles. But when he got to Indiana University, he discovered its Independent Learning Program, which allowed a student to make up his own major in a subject the school didn't offer. As a result, he is the holder of the world's only college degree in enigmatology – the study of puzzles. This included custom-made tutorials in the English and mathematics departments, as well as a thesis on the history of American word puzzles before 1860.

Although his law-school degree was something to fall back on in case his first career choice didn't pan out, Will needn't have worried. His entire working life has been spent as a puzzle editor, including more than ten years at *Games*.

In addition to his *Times* job, Will wears many hats in puzzledom. They include:

Radio Personality He can be heard across the country every Sunday morning with a puzzle on the National Public Radio program *Weekend Edition*.

Tournament Director His American Crossword Puzzle Tournament has been held annually at Stamford, Connecticut's Marriott Hotel since 1978.

International Goodwill Ambassador Will was one of the organizers of the World Puzzle Championships, in which teams from many nations compete on language- and culture-neutral puzzles.

Archivist and Historian Will owns the world's largest collection of puzzle books, magazines, and ephemera. This includes crossword's Holy Grail – an original of the December 1913 edition of *The New York World* that featured the very first crossword.

Puzzle #49 - "Petal Puzzle"
One of many innovative crossword varieties that Will has invented or popularized. The answers, all six-letter words or phrases, are entered clockwise and counterclockwise instead of across and down. Because of the diagram shape, you may find it helpful to rotate the page to read some of the answers.

49
petal puzzle
by will shortz

Fill in this flower with 32 interlocking six-letter words or phrases using the clues below. Enter the words inward from the tips of the petals to the heart of the blossom, one letter per space. Half the words will proceed clockwise, the other half counterclockwise. Work from both sets of clues for a full bloom.

CLOCKWISE
1 TV police drama of 1965-74
2 California peak
3 Trigonometric function
4 No longer active
5 Aqua or ecru, e.g.
6 Instrument of war
7 Prepared beef, in a way
8 Leather worker
9 Something surprising
10 Of a religious season
11 British bishops' apparel
12 Namesakes of an Arthur character
13 Slangy refusal
14 Infer
15 *Moulin de la Galette* painter
16 *Oklahoma!* vehicle

COUNTERCLOCKWISE
1 Forum wear
2 __ Tuesday
3 French sweetheart
4 Informal shoe
5 Overlook en route
6 Elk
7 Aircraft maker
8 Exactly
9 Bent out of shape
10 Former Cambodian premier
11 Big name in toiletries
12 Babysat
13 Talk and talk and talk and . . .
14 More gloomy
15 Flush, in a way
16 Weekly program

Previous Occupation
Mathematics teacher for a vocational high school.

Education
B.S. in mathematics from Penn State.

Crossword Credentials
See below.

If crossword professionals were ranked on their talent-to-ego ratios, Mike Shenk would come out first by a wide margin. His unassuming manner belies an immense talent that has been creating crossword masterpieces for fifteen years. A listing of Mike's noteworthy puzzling achievements would take up many pages; here are just a few of them:

Prizewinning Puzzle His "Alphabet Soup" puzzle, created for a puzzle-constructor contest in 1979, had A PLUS as 1 Across, Z AXIS as the last word Across, and a phrase starting with each of the other letters of the alphabet, *in alphabetical order*, in between.

Anniversary Puzzle To commemorate the 75th anniversary of the first crossword, Mike created a puzzle for *Games* whose center incorporated Arthur Wynne's first crossword of 1913.

The Ultimate Quotation Puzzle A columnist for the *Detroit Free Press* was quoted as saying, "Fame, to me, would be before I die to be 14 Down or 36 Across in a major crossword puzzle." Mike not only used the quote as a theme for a *Games* crossword, but also included the first and last names of the quote's author at 14 Down and 36 Across!

Missing Letter Puzzle A crossword in which the letters of each answer were found in consecutive order in the clues. Asterisks were substituted for the key letters in each clue. For example, the clue "Chocolate source" for COCOA was given as "*h***l*te source."

Audio Puzzle At a convention of the National Puzzler's League, Mike presented the clues verbally rather than on paper. The many diabolical clues included "Barber a bush" for PRUNE (it sounded like "Barbara Bush") and "Capp, Pacino, and others" for ALS (it sounded like "Cappuccino and others").

Maze Puzzle After solving this crossword in the usual manner, a maze was formed. One could start at the top of the diagram, then move to the bottom by traveling only through squares containing one of the letters in LABYRINTH.

Puzzle #50 - "Jumbo Challenger"
A themeless, wide-open giant similar to the "World's Most Ornery" puzzles Mike frequently creates for *Games*. The two principal differences: this one is larger, and there are no "easy" clues to fall back on. The answers cover the widest range of territory, from lively words and phrases to facts old and new. Note also the eye-pleasing pattern typical of Mike's crosswords – a product of his mathematical background.

50

jumbo challenger
by mike shenk

ACROSS
1 Play fellows?
11 Body supporter
18 Road surfaces
26 Play based on *Goodbye to Berlin*
27 Meat-wrapped dish
28 Dostoyevsky novel
29 Jelly-making fruits
30 Y's look-alike
31 Sets out toward
32 Coworker of Mary and Murray
33 Beethoven affliction
35 Gunpowder, for one
36 Widen
38 "Boola boola" cheerer
39 *The Night of the Hunter* screenwriter
41 Stream sediment
42 Place to buy a tie
45 Piece of cake
46 Dig
48 Arrived abundantly
50 Parade entrants
51 Golfer Calvin
52 Lamb products
54 Made worthless
55 Spiral ornament on a column
56 Noted California mill owner
57 Whom gentlemen marry, according to Loos
59 *Queen Anne's Revenge* and others
61 Humble
64 "Mazel __!"
65 In questionable taste
66 Make amends for
70 Monopoly avenue
72 Cage of the movies
74 Soccer position
77 Curly-coated cat
78 Wheaties rival
80 Golden brew
81 Dizzy's horn
82 Virus core
83 Rap-music star
85 Appointed
87 Occupy oneself
89 Leaves
90 Act the harpist
92 Wise guy
93 Favorite
94 Part of QED
95 International understanding
97 Fabric fuzz
99 Traveled, Finn-style
101 Making things happen
103 Fall from grace
104 Biblical "father of many nations"
108 Cohort of Haley and Bolger
109 Stole stuff
110 __ out (supplements)
112 Andy Garcia, for one
116 Ticks off
117 Totalitarian system
120 Monthly expenses
122 Missile setting
123 Calf cry
124 Rochester's river
125 Caustic
127 Starter courses, often
129 Bowie or Bishop
130 Communion wafers
132 Took a shot
134 Battle site of 1777
136 City on Lake Victoria
137 Thurber's dreamer
138 Early horror-film name
140 Court stat
141 Narrow escapes
145 Guiding principles
147 Drugged drink
150 Come to
151 International Red Cross headquarters
152 *The Bicycle Thief* director
156 Pop stars
157 PC parts
158 Pound residents
160 *Eight Is Enough* daughter
161 Debbie and Donald's *Singin' in the Rain* costar
162 Court invitation
164 Bring up
166 Straight-haired dogs, for short
167 Betrayer
168 Hearst's girlfriend
169 *Twin Peaks* prop
170 Hepburn/Tracy comedy
173 Bar concern
174 Continental competitor
176 Papa Doc, for one
179 "Never!"
181 Joining with a mortise
182 Initially
183 United Nations employee
184 Article clarifications
185 Dispositions
186 Bardot, e.g.

DOWN
1 Compose a letter, in a way
2 Argon or neon
3 Tony-winning play of '81
4 Fairy queen
5 West Pt., e.g.
6 Studio creations
7 Weaken
8 Vanity
9 Southern senator
10 Accompaniment for an MS
11 Aggressive campaigns
12 School dance
13 Emma Woodhouse's creator
14 More devious
15 Service requirements
16 Witness' oath
17 Issues
18 Sullivan Award candidates
19 Barbering tool
20 Like some marshes
21 Hole up
22 Pitches
23 Firefighters' catcher
24 "It's __" (Carole King tune)
25 Angler's catch
34 '89 Meryl/Roseanne film
37 "__ Men" (Porter tune)
40 Give a chance
43 Two hearts, e.g.
44 Quiet
45 Arrives
47 Coup target
49 Discovered
51 Punch, for one
53 *Memoirs of a Bank Robber* author
55 Parish heads
56 Dress sizes at Lane Bryant
58 __ a pin
59 Least colorful
60 Request of Rhonda
61 A costar of Rock
62 Fabricate
63 Darkroom bath
65 Dressed à la *Animal House*
67 Extra charge
68 Doctrine
69 Expunge
71 NFL owner Hunt
73 Completing strokes
74 Fonzie, for one
75 Bloopers show offering
76 "All Alone __" (Brenda Lee tune)
79 Letter-of-the-law follower
81 Like some traffic
84 Charlie and others
86 Sprays graffiti on
88 Ticket takers, at times

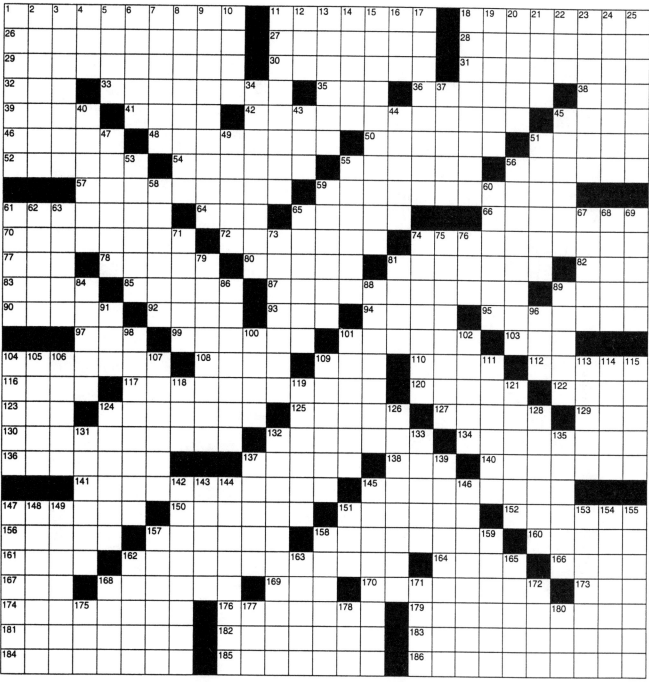

89 Trivial Pursuit edition
91 __-jongg
96 First of three X's
98 News caster?
100 Friend's address?
101 Overly precious
102 Late-night host's family
104 *La Dolce Vita* actress
105 Marconi collaborator

106 Gasp, perhaps
107 Account's amounts
109 Baguette features
111 Queen Anne's house
113 Popular old theater name
114 Straighten
115 Itinerant
118 Article written by Molière
119 Remove slack from
121 Two-page story

124 Features of a Hawthorne house
126 Fit in
128 Buffalo players
131 Annoy the comic
132 Picks up a hitcher
133 Meter?
135 *College Bowl* question
137 Car choices
139 Raven call
142 Salary
143 Sows

144 *Great Expectations* character
145 Stadium flyers
146 Subtotal additive
147 Seek greener pastures
148 Think-tank thinkers
149 Profess
151 Rubber cement, e.g.
153 Quarantine
154 '60s Chevys
155 Responds to a ring

157 Sumner on *Knots Landing*
158 #1 Temptations tune
159 Island wrap
162 Implied
163 Tag cry
165 All rival
168 Pebbles' pet
171 Colony members
172 Lacking locks
175 Baseballers Cey or Santo
177 Did lunch
178 Enzyme suffix
180 Dear old one?

1

C	O	I	N		H	M	O	S		E	S	P	S
A	N	T	E		A	I	D	E		G	I	L	A
S	C	H	W	A	R	Z	E	N	E	G	G	E	R
T	E	E	S	U	P			A	M	A	N	D	A
		M	N	O		S	T	I	R				
J	A	N	E	T		S	P	O	T		B	A	T
E	D	E	N		R	O	A	R	S		E	R	E
F	E	E		D	O	R	I	S		G	A	L	E
F	E	D		A	M	E	N		O	R	S	O	N
		B	R	A	N		A	L	I				
A	T	R	A	I	N			D	I	S	N	E	Y
L	A	S	T	A	C	T	I	O	N	H	E	R	O
D	I	V	E		E	A	R	P		A	M	I	D
A	L	P	S		S	P	A	T		M	O	N	A

2

L	I	L		S	I	C		J	A	M	B		L	B	J
I	D	I		B	O	R	O		E	R	I	E		O	O	O
V	A	N	B	U	R	E	N		F	I	L	L	M	O	R	E
	C	A	S	T		S	O	F	A			O	K	E	Y
E	N	O	C	H		G	O	R	E		H	M	O
P	O	L	K		T	Y	L	E	R		C	A	R	T	E	R
A	N	N		C	O	P	E		S	O	L	D		A	B	C
	F	L	Y		H	O	P		I	N	F	R	A
M	A	L	I		G	R	A	N	T		S	O	T	O
N	I	X	O	N		O	O	M		C	O	D
O	N	E		T	I	T	O		G	A	I	N		J	F	K
W	I	L	S	O	N		S	A	U	N	A		L	A	L	O
	A	N	C		E	M	M	Y		F	O	C	U	S
A	C	L	U		A	V	I	S		B	O	N	K
C	O	O	L	I	D	G	E		H	A	R	R	I	S	O	N
H	B	O		B	R	E	L		O	V	I	D		O	W	N
E	S	P		M	U	S	T		E	G	G		N	E	W

3

T	I	E	R		A	M	E	N		M	O	N	A		S	M	O	G
O	G	L	E		P	O	G	O		A	B	E	L		T	A	X	I
R	O	S	S	P	E	R	O	T		B	I	L	L	G	A	T	E	S
S	T	A	T	U	R	E		N	N	E		L	O	W	R	E	N	T
		S	T	Y		N	O	E	L	S		T	E	M
L	O	T	U	S		L	O	W	B	L	O	W		N	A	S	A	L
U	T	E	P		P	I	T		A	I	M		N	A	M	E
S	T	D		S	T	E	V	E	M	A	R	T	I	N		L	I	E
H	O	T	H	E	A	D		R	Y	E		S	C	H	O	L	A	R
	U	A	R		A	G	O			L	A	Y
B	E	R	M	U	D	A		S	U	N		A	V	E	R	R	E	D
U	R	N		M	O	R	L	E	Y	S	A	F	E	R		I	V	E
M	I	E	S		W	O	E		T	A	X		A	D	E	E
P	E	R	K	S		W	A	I	T	F	O	R		W	I	E	L	D
	I	T	S		P	S	A	L	M		F	O	R
S	H	A	N	A	N	A		O	U	I		R	I	O	L	O	B	O
T	I	P	O	N	E	I	L	L		N	E	I	L	S	I	M	O	N
E	R	O	S		A	R	I	D		C	R	O	C		F	A	D	E
P	E	P	E		K	Y	L	E		H	A	T	H		T	R	E	S

4

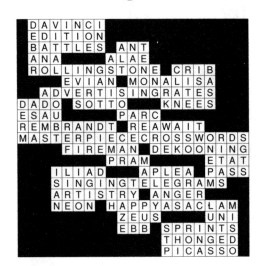

D	A	V	I	N	C	I
E	D	I	T	I	O	N
B	A	T	T	L	E	S		A	N	T
A	N	A		A	L	A	E
R	O	L	L	I	N	G	S	T	O	N	E		C	R	I	B
	E	V	I	A	N		M	O	N	A	L	I	S	A
A	D	V	E	R	T	I	S	I	N	G	R	A	T	E	S
D	A	D	O		S	O	T	T	O		K	N	E	E	S
E	S	A	U		P	A	R	C
R	E	M	B	R	A	N	D	T		R	E	A	W	A	I	T
M	A	S	T	E	R	P	I	E	C	E	C	R	O	S	S	W	O	R	D	S
	F	I	R	E	M	A	N		D	E	K	O	O	N	I	N	G
	P	R	A	M			E	T	A	T
I	L	I	A	D		A	P	L	E	A		P	A	S	S
S	I	N	G	I	N	G	T	E	L	E	G	R	A	M	S
A	R	T	I	S	T	R	Y		A	N	G	E	R
N	E	O	N		H	A	P	P	Y	A	S	A	C	L	A	M
Z	E	U	S			U	N	I
E	B	B		S	P	R	I	N	T	S
	T	H	O	N	G	E	D
	P	I	C	A	S	S	O

5

S	O	N	Y	A	L	I	V	E		B	L	O	C
A	R	E	A	C	O	D	E	S		D	R	I	V	E
I	N	C	L	E	M	E	N	T		R	A	V	E	N
D	A	T	E		A	S	U			A	V	E	R	T
I	T	A		A	N	T	E	S		P	O	L	A	R
T	E	R	R	I			T	E	E		I	L	A
		A	L	I	V	E	A	N	D	W	E	L	L
L	M	N		M	E	S	S	Y		I	R	S
D	E	A	D	M	A	N	S	H	A	N	D
E	A	N		O	N	A			F	E	L	L	S
A	P	A	P	A		L	O	C	A	L		O	A	T
D	Y	L	A	N		B	O	B		L	U	N	E
S	E	I	N	E		R	E	S	I	D	E	N	C	E
E	A	V	E	D		E	S	T	R	A	N	G	E	D
T	R	E	S		D	E	A	D	P	O	E	T	S

6

E	D	D	A		D	E	C	A		R	A	T	S
P	E	R	R	Y	M	A	S	O	N		S	O	N	A	T	A
I	F	Y	O	U	A	R	E	N	T		T	A	S	T	E	S
	S	L	Y			F	I	R	E	D	W	I	T	H
	G	L	E	E		C	H	E		E	R	S	E
A	R	E		H	A	I	R	P	I	N		R	A	L	E
R	E	F	R	A	I	N	S		A	L	E		A	M	O	S
R	E	T	A	K	E		E	L	L			A	M	S
E	N	T	H	U	S	I	A	S	M	Y	O	U	L	L	B	E
A	B	U		L	T	D		B	R	O	G	A	N
R	A	R	A		F	L	U		I	R	O	N	W	A	R	E
S	Y	N	D		L	I	B	E	L	E	E		M	D	S
	D	E	A	N		T	K	O		S	I	S	I
F	I	R	E	D	W	I	T	H			F	O	R
B	R	I	D	G	E		E	N	T	H	U	S	I	A	S	M
I	M	B	U	E	D		D	I	A	G	N	O	S	T	I	C
A	S	P	S		S	C	O	T		H	A	N	S

7

```
    BATS   AMBIT   UHF
ACROBAT  MIRTH   MARC
CAESURA  BLASE   ARIAS
CUDS   BELA   ACE   DEBT
  LHASA  YEGG  OLA  DBA
CIO  IRAE   REPROS   GAL
AFT  LOLL   ORAN   NORGE
TLC  TUBE   BALI   ADEER
OOHS  SET   ELMS   KEEP
  WITHER   TAD  GRETNA
  ELEE  THEN  ARE  OTTO
CRIER  BEEF   SELA  OCT
AMPLE  RAVI   SEAM  MHO
BCE  ADOREE   ONTO  ADE
APP  TEC  ELMO  ERATO
LUPE  RCA  DENT   BOLA
AGENA  OZAWA  ASABELL
  GROW  LOGAN  PELISSE
  SSE  IVORY  SALE
```

8

```
FIRST  DERN  ASPS  BOSC
ITHEE  ELIA  POSY  KUNTA
GOODTIMECHAPLIN  AFTER
  ALCOVE  POI  CARFARE
SYDNEY   REID  LEAPED
NEWSY  ASTERN  CREEL
AME   BLOODYTYLERMOORE
FEED  OILED  OAST  CZAR
UNBOARDED  BAUM  ALANS
  ULNA  TONGUE  DIRGE
ROBBEDNEROTOPAYANKA
DENTE  EATERS  SEPT
OSSIE  THES  POTATOBUD
TEEN  AMIE  DATER  NOPE
STAGEDOORCARSONS  OFA
  EVIAN  ABATED  MANON
ANADEM  ALIT  HIDERS
MARINES  DYE  BLUISH
IDEST  DEMPSEYINTHEBOX
NINOS  ARES  ATRI  ARABY
ORAN  KENO  NEAT  PEREZ
```

9

```
GAGA  MEAD  STACK
ARAM  ORNO  PELLE
FAME  TOTO  INCAN
FRENCHDIRECTOR
EAT  AYE  BYE  HIT
STEAD  SKEE  MONA
  DIA  ILL  ALEX
  JAZZVIOLINIST
MOLE  ADS  DUN
AHAS  NIKE  REDAN
CNN  GTO  ASS  EGO
  PATRICKSTEWART
TALIA  IOTA  AREA
AUDEN  ELON  STET
BLAST  SAND  POSE
```

10

```
ICEMAN  DISBAR  TNT
LIKETO  INSOLE  ROE
LIGHTNINGRODS  INN
  TASTE  MAEWEST
MAMA  THROE  EASE
AVE  MOE  PLANKTONS
RESHIP  BELIE  TUSK
CRAIG  BIN  MAO  TEY
  CHURCHYARDS
MPH  TRY  OAT  IOWAN
ERIE  DATUM  SUBARU
DOGPOUNDS  REM  KIN
  THOU  SEMIS  DEAN
WRESTLE  INANE
OAR  PARKINGMETERS
ECU  UNLACE  EXETER
STP  TEETER  STRAYS
```

11

```
SAMBA  ARENA  IMPALA
ALIEN  DAMON  SNEAKER
WORLDRECORD  TSARINA
STET  APER  RIOT  KNOB
  ENTRY  ERRED
OCELOTS  STAMPALBUM
ROBINS  ELATE  NOONE
COALS  TRINI  REGATTA
ANNA  BEARD  EARL  HOT
  CHEESESINGLES
TEC  ORNE  TOSEE  HALO
ALLERGY  HONUS  CASED
GEENA  DONEE  SALTED
SCOTCHTAPE  STREAKS
  EERIE  POPUP
PEAS  LESS  ADIN  MISS
ALLTIME  FLYINGDISCS
CLEAVES  OVINE  ILLAT
SECRET  RINGS  MEETS
```

12

```
LOAD  BEES  ADOS  GAMES
ERLE  ETTU  DOVES  OMANI
TALC  ATTN  DRINK  OUTER
ONEOFTHEBLOODTYPES
  GYRATE  AINT  LAYERED
ATO  GTO  HAMAN  ELI
ABATH  JOHNNYHARTCOMIC
CAMEO  ARESO  ORK  RUEDE
ASI  MINIS  VARY  TOTTED
RIGA  REO  DENS  ORAL
  CASSETTEALTERNATIVE
  CONS  RBIS  OLD  EARS
ALLELE  PROS  STIES  DAT
SAINT  SEA  TITAN  UNITE
THEDIAMONDSTATE  BISON
ETO  LENTO  ANE  WAN
PINBALL  WELD  CARESS
  INITIALSOFMRHUTTON
EBERT  ELLIS  ALII  EINE
BONDS  DIANE  SVEN  ELAM
BOSSY  ERGS  TIDE  NERO
```

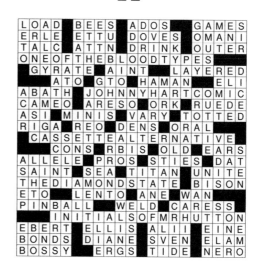

13

14

15

16

17

18

19

20

21

22

23

24

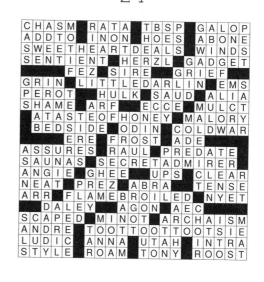

25

26

27

28

```
COT . DICED . COUPS . SRA
APR AIRIER OASES SQIN
SQUIDMARKS GREATSQUAT
ARENOSE DEEDS QUASI
. TRU ALMOND GUAR
SUPREMEQUART PARADES
OREOS RUNTS WIDOW CES
FATS TRACE RENEW CRAM
ALE PEACHYQUEEN GLOBE
FRANK UMPS TROWEL
BONIEST SOAPY QUONSET
AVERSE SPRY CURVE
HEXES CHEESEQUAKE ESS
ARTS SPINS LUNDI ATTU
IDO INAPT WOOER EQUAL
OFCLASS CAPTAINQUIRK
QUIP LOREAL OUI
ACURA APORT ATALOSS
QUITCARSON QUOTETAILS
URNS CEASE ENTIRE LUG
IBN TATER DEBTS YET
```

29

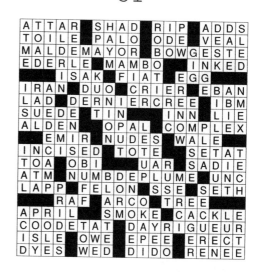

```
SLAM COLT . CREME
PAPA AVER HADAT
CHECKMATE IMAGO
ARCANE VITAMIN
SKOAL ZINC
POGO CHOKED
ARAB TOOL APILE
LURID ALA TATES
ADIEU DOVE LEEK
SEARCH GAPE
KATY ISLAM
CAPABLE TAIPEI
ALIBI TABHUNTER
MOTEL OGRE ELSE
STALL NEAT RYES
```

30

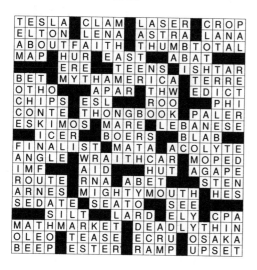

```
WAR JONAH TRASH
OWE OPERAS RANCID
RAG CARUSO ANDREA
TRACKLIGHTING ARM
HENCE SSS STOP
SYSTS TOPIC
LOS SHOPS MOTHER
ART HABITAT SAPPY
MARCO ERASE TRACE
ATEAR DOMINUM DON
SETSTO PATTI STY
CUSPS NOOSE
MOHS THO TERSE
ESL FIELDOFDREAMS
ACIDIC DEGREE BAS
TAMORA SPREES ASA
ROWEL TEEMS THY
```

31

```
ATTAR SHAD RIP ADDS
TOILE PALO ODE VEAL
MALDEMAYOR BOWGESTE
EDERLE MAMBO INKED
ISAK FIAT EGG
IRAN DUO CRIER EBAN
LAD DERNIERCREE IBM
SUEDE TIN INN LIE
ALDEN OPAL COMPLEX
EMIR NUDES WALE
INCISED TOTE SETAT
TOA OBI UAR SADIE
ATM NUMBDEPLUME UNC
LAPP FELON SSE SETH
RAF ARCO TREE
APRIL SMOKE CACKLE
COODETAT DAYRIGUEUR
ISLE OWE EPEE ERECT
DYES WED DIDO RENEE
```

32

```
TESLA CLAM LASER CROP
ELTON LENA ASTRA LANA
ABOUTFAITH THUMBTOTAL
MAP HUR EAST ABAT
ERE TEENS ISHTAR
BET MYTHAMERICA TERRE
OTHO APAR THW EDICT
CHIPS ESL ROO PHI
CONTE THONGBOOK PALER
ESKIMOS MARE LEBANESE
ICER BOERS BLAB
FINALIST MATA ACOLYTE
ANGLE WRAITHCAR MOPED
IMF AID HUT AGAPE
ROUTE RNA ABET STEN
ARNES MIGHTYMOUTH HES
SEDATE SEATO SEE
SILT LARD ELY CPA
MATHMARKET DEADLYTHIN
OLEO TEASE ECRU OSAKA
BEEP ESTER RAMP UPSET
```

33

```
EOS MOTH SSTS
ANTS ELBE RATON
RIOT DESI ATARI
LOVEBUG DEMERIT
NEARS KISMET
MIAOU TENONS
TIBET UMBER VOW
AVER PIQUE BETA
TAG JESUS ARRAY
ANIMAL ATONE
NICEST STARE
BLANKET SPIKING
AINGE AZUR UCLA
SMELT VINE PEAR
HOWE EASY RIB
```

34

ACROSS 1. PIERCE (two definitions) 4. SECOND HAND (two definitions) 10. ADDERS (two definitions) 11. DINING ROOM (hidden) 13. MINUTE MAN (two definitions) 14. READING (two definitions) 15. CHELSEA (anagram of *Lee* and *Chas.*) 16. BANDIT (homophone of *banned it*) 19. STEAM (hidden) 21. TIERS (homophone of *tears*) 23. G + HOST 24. OSCARS (anagram of *Across*) 26. TRESTLE (anagram of *letters*) 30. REIGNED (pun on *rained*) 31. BELA + BORED 32. MARIONETTE (homophone of *marry Annette*) 33. CAN CAN (two definitions) 34. RINGMASTER (two definitions) 35. SEANCE (anagram of *Seneca*)

DOWN 1. PHARMACIST (homophone of *farm assist*) 2. END + ANGERED 3. CURATES (anagram of *sure act*) 5. EVIAN (*naive* backwards) 6. OMICRON (anagram of *moronic*) 7. DE-GRADING (pun) 8. A + DON + IS 9. DAM + AGE 12. IMP + ART 16. B-LESS (pun) 17. COSTA RICAN (anagram of *an acrostic*) 18. AT + TEN + DANCE 20. M + IS + IN + FORM 22. SETTLE (*Seattle* minus *a*) 25. ANDREWS (anagram of *wanders*) 27. EMBRACE (anagram of *Reb came*) 28. TREMOR (anagram of *Mr. Rote*) 29. GI + BRAN 31. BUTTE (homophone of *beaut*)

35

36

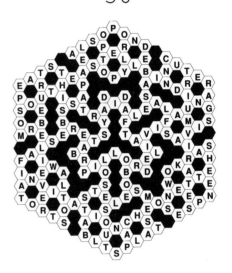

37

38

39

```
TOFFEES LEAVE DIMER
UKULELE APRIL EMILE
BREAKFASTATTIFFANYS
BALM NUTRIA REMISE
   BIB NICE AER VIN
NAKEDLUNCH ACES EAT
ESE LURIE LIES ERNS
BAR ERG WORRIES
URAL BEGGARSBANQUET
LUTED ALINE DUNNE
AMOVEABLEFEAST ESTA
   EILEENS OAS TIS
GOAL MANN BURST ORE
RUN RAMA LASTSUPPER
ITT ENS MORI ONE
PLASMA SARONG ABAS
PICNICATHANGINGROCK
EVIES MARIE SEALANE
REDES TRENT TRYSTED
```

40

```
ASTARTE HAREM SUSANNS
STALEST AROLE CRUSOES
POLICEOFFICER REPIVOT
SLIGO UTA CCC EDENS
SONLESS ETUI OREL
MOVIEACTORRON SIRS
FEDERAL RETRY MAC SET
ALANS VETOES CANO TRA
CURT HELI SLR BAHAI
ELK CHRYSLERCAR AMEND
BLAH STADIUM SLUR BVI
SOLAR FIRSTPLANET
CRUMB LAY PNOM GEER
ODE OLIN PLATTS BURRO
PEP NAE POOPO TAUNTON
ERIC PRESSGARMENTS
GOLD LETS ERECTOR
HUMPH FUL GAS HOVEL
ONEPAIR DUPLICATECOPY
HONESTY ODIUM DARKLES
OSTRAVA SEEMS MISSILE
```

41

```
GOTCHA ARMCHAIR
AVALON SEAHORSE
RETOLD SCREECHY
BRENDA OATES
STREWN CLIP GEM
   ATTILA AURA
ETCETERA LAMARR
SHARE ETA HOVEL
SENORA ELDORADO
AMIS BADGUY
YET RAMP STACKS
   MILER THRALL
ALCAPONE PEORIA
BOOKENDS ARMANI
CUTENESS NEATEN
```

42

```
ADRIFT PASTA ATWT
TOOTOO AFLAT TIER
INTERMITTENT ETTU
TEEM STOPGAP TBS
   TALENT ECLAT
TITTERED TATTERS
ATEASE TAUTEST
RHETT STENTOR ACT
TOTS STANTON STAR
STE SPATTER LOTTO
   ROTATES TOILET
ACTUATE TWITTERS
BLOTS EGOIST
JOT HAMLETS SOFT
ETTA HITTHEBOTTLE
CHET ATONE TOATEE
TERM TENOR UPTOWN
```

43

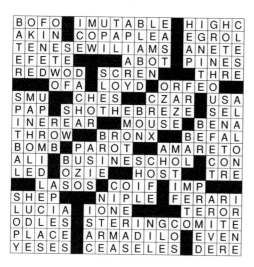

```
BOFO IMUTABLE HIGHC
AKIN COPAPLEA EGROL
TENESEWILLIAMS ANETE
EFETE ABOT PINES
REDWOD SCREN THRE
   OFA LOYD ORFEO
SMU CHES CZAR USA
PAP SHOTHEBREZE SEL
INEREAR MOUSE BENA
THROW BRONX BEFAL
BOMB PAROT AMARETO
ALI BUSINESCHOL CON
LED OZIE HOST TRE
   LASOS COIF IMP
SHEP NIPLE FERARI
LUCIA IONE TEROR
ODLES STERINGCOMITE
PLACE ARMADILO EVEN
YESES CEASELES DERE
```

44

```
SIMS ALBATROSS CANVAS
KNIT COUGHDROP ORIENT
ESSDOUBLEUAKAY IMPEDE
DIS AMBLED OAF PAIR
ADM SEES FIEND ALIEN
DEADEND SMOKY VALET
DORIS TEEGEEIEFF COT
LUCK CLINGY SORT THAI
ETH CHEAT BOOB RHETT
   SHEER POOR MORSEL
EMICEEKAYEWYEEMOUESSE
MOHAWK EELS MANSE
POEMS WISP BIZET COB
TRAP PERM OMELET DOFF
YER ATEEANDTEE TURFS
   TRIAD AEONS LAYBACK
GLEAM ELMER DULL LAI
RANK ODO BLITHE RMN
ATWILL PEEGEETHIRTEEN
PHYSED ESCALATOR WERE
HEEHEE STOPSHORT AFAR
```

45

```
P A R I A H S ■ ■ G A R A G E
A L U M N A E ■ N U M E R A L
D E S P I T E ■ O N E B A L L
S C H E M E S ■ I G N O B L E
■ ■ L A T ■ P R A T T L E R
A P E ■ T O O L ■ D A T E R S
C R E T E ■ V A N I L L A ■
E Y R E ■ C A N O N ■ E G G S
■ I N S O L E S ■ U S U A L
D A E D A L ■ T E S S ■ E L Y
E S T E L L E S ■ H A W ■
S P A R T A N ■ M A G I C A L
P I L E A T E ■ A V E R A G E
O R E S T E S ■ R E N E G E S
T E S T E D ■ ■ E N T R E E S
```

46

```
A L E X K A R R A S ■ S H O G U N
M O V I E D E A L S ■ T O B A G O
B L I N D E D B Y T H E L I G H T
L I N G ■ L I B ■ S O N Y ■ E S E
E T C ■ A E G I S ■ L O W S ■
S A E N S ■ T A R S ■ A T S E A
■ A S T I ■ G O T A R O U N D
D O C T O R M Y E Y E S ■ P O N D
E C O ■ C A P O ■ A R I Z ■ M I O
B E A S ■ D O U B L E V I S I O N
R A S P B E R R Y ■ D E N Y ■
A N T A L ■ T E E D ■ G R A S S
■ M E N U ■ S O L E S ■ T A N
J I G ■ S O N S ■ Z O E ■ B O L O
I C A N S E E C L E A R L Y N O W
L E M U E L ■ A U N T I E M A M E
T R E N D S ■ D I S H E V E L E D
```

47

```
G E T I T ■ F A R A D ■ S T R A D A
A C H O O ■ B O R A G E ■ F R O M A N
W H I S K Y A G O G O L ■ P I S A N S
K O S ■ Y A D ■ W A R A N D P I Z Z A
■ C O R G I ■ A Y E ■ O N E A
A L B A ■ R U N T Y ■ S E A L ■
T O L S T O Y S R U S ■ D I S N E Y
M O O C O W ■ C U R A C A O ■ H A L O
■ K O A N ■ T H E I G O R B E A V E R
L E M ■ E L I O ■ R I E N ■ A C E
O D E S S A G O O D O N E ■ S E R T
K I R K ■ B E L T O N E ■ A U R O R A
I N S I D E ■ C O M R A D E O N I N
■ A L U M ■ M E E T S ■ S E C T
W A R M ■ R E B ■ D O O N E ■
B E B O P B E L U G A ■ N R A ■ C O P
A S A B E E ■ B Y E B Y E B O R Z O I
R E S I S T ■ A U T O E D ■ M E A N T
B R E N T S ■ S P A W N ■ I P R A Y
```

48

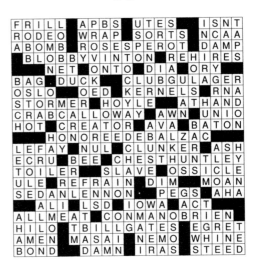

```
F R I L L ■ A P B S ■ U T E S ■ I S N T
R O D E O ■ W R A P ■ S O R T S ■ N C A A
A B O M B ■ R O S E S P E R O T ■ D A M P
■ B L O B B Y V I N T O N ■ R E H I R E S
■ N E T ■ O N T O ■ D I A ■ O R Y ■
B A G ■ D U C K ■ C L U B G U L A G E R
O S L O ■ O E D ■ K E R N E L S ■ R N A
S T O R M E R ■ H O Y L E ■ A T H A N D
C R A B C A L L O W A Y ■ A W N ■ U N I O
H O T ■ C R E A T O R ■ A V A ■ B A T O N
H O N O R E E D E B A L Z A C
L E F A Y ■ N U L ■ C L U N K E R ■ A S H
E C R U ■ B E E ■ C H E S T H U N T L E Y
T O I L E R ■ S L A V E ■ O S S I C L E
U L E ■ R E F R A I N ■ D I M ■ M O A N
S E D A N L E N N O N ■ P E G S ■ A H A
A L I ■ L S D ■ I O W A ■ A C T
A L L M E A T ■ C O N M A N O B R I E N
H I L O ■ T B I L L G A T E S ■ E G R E T
A M E N ■ M A S A I ■ N E M O ■ W H I N E
B O N D ■ D A M N ■ I R A S ■ S T E E D
```

49

50

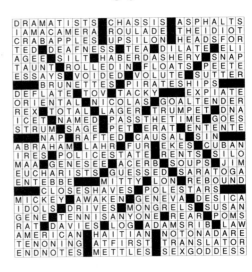

```
D R A M A T I S T S ■ C H A S S I S ■ A S P H A L T S
I A M A C A M E R A ■ R O U L A D E ■ T H E I D I O T
C R A B A P P L E S ■ U P S I L O N ■ H E A D S F O R
T E D ■ D E A F N E S S ■ T E A ■ D I L A T E ■ E L I
A G E E ■ S I L T ■ H A B E R D A S H E R Y ■ S N A P
T A U N T ■ R O L L E D I N ■ F L O A T S ■ P E E T E
E S S A Y S ■ V O I D E D ■ V O L U T E ■ S U T T E R
■ B R U N E T T E S ■ P I R A T E S H I P S ■
D E F L A T E ■ T O V ■ T A C K Y ■ E X P I A T E
O R I E N T A L ■ N I C O L A S ■ G O A L T E N D E R
R E X ■ T O T A L ■ L A G E R ■ T R U M P E T ■ D N A
I C E T ■ N A M E D ■ P A S S T H E T I M E ■ G O E S
S T R U M ■ S A G E ■ P E T ■ E R A T ■ E N T E N T E
■ N A P ■ R A F T E D ■ C A U S A L ■ S I N ■
A B R A H A M ■ L A H R ■ F U R ■ E K E S ■ C U B A N
I R E S ■ P O L I C E S T A T E ■ R E N T S ■ S I L O
M A A ■ G E N E S E E ■ A C E R B ■ S O U P S ■ J I M
E U C H A R I S T S ■ G U E S S E D ■ S A R A T O G A
E N T E B B E ■ M I T T Y ■ L O N ■ R E B O U N D
■ C L O S E S H A V E S ■ P O L E S T A R S ■
M I C K E Y ■ A W A K E N ■ G E N E V A ■ D E S I C A
I D O L S ■ D R I V E S ■ M O N G R E L S ■ S U S A N
G E N E ■ T E N N I S A N Y O N E ■ R E A R ■ P O M S
R A T ■ D A V I E S ■ L O G ■ A D A M S R I B ■ L A W
A M E R I C A N ■ H A I T I A N ■ N O T O N A D A R E
T E N O N I N G ■ A T F I R S T ■ T R A N S L A T O R
E N D N O T E S ■ M E T T L E S ■ S E X G O D D E S S
```

TIMES BOOKS CROSSWORD ORDER FORM

VOL	ISBN	QUANTITY	PRICE	TOTAL PRICE

L.A. Times Sunday Crosswords
Witty, contemporary puzzles from the pages of the Los Angeles Times.

VOL	ISBN	QUANTITY	PRICE	TOTAL PRICE
1	91910-6		$7.50	
2	91911-4		$7.50	
3	91915-7		$8.00	
4	91916-5		$7.50	
5	91917-3		$7.50	
6	91918-1		$7.50	
7	91919-X		$8.00	
8	91920-3		$7.50	
9	92227-1		$7.50	
10	92228-X		$7.50	
11	92229-8		$8.00	
12	92230-1		$8.00	

Washington Post Sunday Crosswords
N.Y. Times-quality puzzles from the nation's capital.

VOL	ISBN	QUANTITY	PRICE	TOTAL PRICE
1	91933-5		$8.00	
2	91934-3		$7.50	
3	92109-7		$7.50	

N.Y. Times Daily Crosswords
America's favorite mental exercise!

VOL	ISBN	QUANTITY	PRICE	TOTAL PRICE
27	91879-7		$7.50	
28	91899-1		$7.00	
29	91937-8		$7.00	
30	91997-1		$7.50	
31	92043-0		$8.00	
32	92082-1		$7.50	
33	92183-6		$7.50	
34	92209-3		$7.50	
35	92270-0		$7.50	
36	92340-5		$8.00	

N.Y. Times Sunday Crosswords
The standard by which other crosswords have been judged for more than 50 years.

VOL	ISBN	QUANTITY	PRICE	TOTAL PRICE
10	91083-4		$7.50	
11	91115-6		$7.50	
12	91166-0		$8.00	
13	91191-1		$7.50	
14	91681-6		$7.50	
15	91781-2		$7.50	
16	91839-8		$7.50	
17	91878-9		$7.50	
18	92268-9		$7.50	
19	92083-X		$7.50	

N.Y. Times Toughest Crosswords
The "toughest of the tough" from the Times puzzle page.

VOL	ISBN	QUANTITY	PRICE	TOTAL PRICE
1	91694-8		$8.00	
2	91828-2		$8.00	
3	91912-2		$8.00	
4	92178-X		$9.00	

Crossword Omnibus Volumes
Your best puzzling values— each with 200 crosswords, at a great price!

Will Weng Sunday Crossword Omnibus

VOL	ISBN	QUANTITY	PRICE	TOTAL PRICE
1	91300-0		$10.00	
2	91645-X		$10.00	
3	91935-1		$10.00	

N.Y. Times Daily Crossword Omnibus

VOL	ISBN	QUANTITY	PRICE	TOTAL PRICE
1	91094-X		$10.00	
2	91018-4		$10.00	
3	91066-4		$10.00	
4	91117-2		$10.00	
5	91708-1		$10.00	
6	92124-0		$10.00	

N.Y. Times Sunday Crossword Omnibus

VOL	ISBN	QUANTITY	PRICE	TOTAL PRICE
1	91139-3		$10.00	
2	91791-X		$10.00	
3	91936-X		$10.00	

N.Y. Times SkillBuilder Crosswords
The first crossword series in three levels of difficulty—specially designed to teach beginners the "rules of the game" and improve puzzlers' skills.

One-star Beginner Level

VOL	ISBN	QUANTITY	PRICE	TOTAL PRICE
1	92302-2		$8.00	

Two-star Apprentice Level

VOL	ISBN	QUANTITY	PRICE	TOTAL PRICE
1	92303-0		$8.00	

Three-star Strategist Level

VOL	ISBN	QUANTITY	PRICE	TOTAL PRICE
1	92304-9		$8.00	

Acrostic Puzzles
Change-of-pace puzzles with a literary flavor that reveal interesting quotations when completed.

N.Y. Times Acrostics

VOL	ISBN	QUANTITY	PRICE	TOTAL PRICE
3	91116-4		$7.50	
4	91302-7		$7.50	

N.Y. Times Acrostic Omnibus

VOL	ISBN	QUANTITY	PRICE	TOTAL PRICE
2	91994-7		$8.00	
3	92362-6		$8.50	

L.A. Times Duo-Crostics

VOL	ISBN	QUANTITY	PRICE	TOTAL PRICE
1	92225-5		$8.00	

GAMES Magazine Crosswords and Word Games
Lively, solver-friendly puzzles from America's most fascinating puzzle magazine.

World's Most Ornery Crosswords

VOL	ISBN	QUANTITY	PRICE	TOTAL PRICE
	92081-3		$13.00	

Giant Book of Games

VOL	ISBN	QUANTITY	PRICE	TOTAL PRICE
	91951-3		$13.00	

Will Shortz's Best Brain Busters

VOL	ISBN	QUANTITY	PRICE	TOTAL PRICE
	91952-1		$11.00	

Games' Best Pencil Puzzles

VOL	ISBN	QUANTITY	PRICE	TOTAL PRICE
	92080-5		$11.00	

Brain Twisters from the First World Puzzle Championships

VOL	ISBN	QUANTITY	PRICE	TOTAL PRICE
	92146-1		$11.00	

Puzzles For Kids
Start your favorite youngster on a lifetime of brainbuilding fun! (For ages 7 to 14)

GAMES Magazine Kids' Giant Book of Games

VOL	ISBN	QUANTITY	PRICE	TOTAL PRICE
	92199-2		$12.00	

GAMES Magazine Riddlers for Kids

VOL	ISBN	QUANTITY	PRICE	TOTAL PRICE
	92385-5		$11.00	

Cryptic Crosswords
Sophisticated puzzles in the British style, using American English.

GAMES Magazine Cryptic Crosswords

VOL	ISBN	QUANTITY	PRICE	TOTAL PRICE
	91999-8		$8.00	

Crosswords from The Nation

VOL	ISBN	QUANTITY	PRICE	TOTAL PRICE
1	92012-0		$7.50	
2	92013-9		$7.50	
3	92031-7		$7.50	
4	92032-5		$7.50	
5	92033-3		$7.50	
6	92034-1		$7.50	

N.Y. Times Puns and Anagrams

VOL	ISBN	QUANTITY	PRICE	TOTAL PRICE
1	92271-9		$7.50	

N.Y. Times Crossword Dictionary
The revised edition of the classic reference book for crossword fans.

VOL	ISBN	QUANTITY	PRICE	TOTAL PRICE
	91131-8		$21.00	

Additional Times Books crossword puzzle books are available through your local bookstore, or fill out this coupon and return to:

RANDOM HOUSE, INC., 400 HAHN ROAD, WESTMINSTER, MD 21157. ATTN: ORDER PROCESSING

TO ORDER CALL TOLL-FREE
1-800-793-BOOK

☐ Enclosed is my check or money order payable to Times Books

☐ Charge my account with: ☐ American Express   ☐ Visa   ☐ MasterCard

EXP DATE (MO/YR)

Price applies to U.S. and territories only.
In Canada write Random House of Canada,
5390 Ambler Drive, Mississauga, Ontario.
(Prices subject to change.)

Please send me copies of the crossword books I have checked off, in the amounts indicated.

Name (please print) _____   Signature _____

Address _____   City _____   State _____   Zip _____

_____ Total Books

Total Dollars $ _____

Sales Tax $ _____
(Where applicable)

Postage and
Handling $ __2.00__

Total Enclosed $ _____